UNUSUAL ORCAS ISLAND

GHOST STORIES AND OTHER LEGENDS FROM THE GEM OF THE SAN JUANS

by **JOSEPH W. REIGEL**

ORCAS ISLAND HISTORY PRESS
EASTSOUND, WASH.

BOOKS BY JOSEPH W. REIGEL

SHIPWRECKS OF THE SAN JUANS

A complete history of maritime disasters in the San Juan Islands, from the earliest schooners to the naval aircraft of World War II.

MYSTERIOUS SAN JUAN ISLAND

A collection of strange accounts and bizarre history from the famed "Pig War island," including UFO encounters, sasquatch sightings, ghosts, and everything in-between.

Contents

BOOKS BY JOSEPH W. REIGEL

SHIPWRECKS OF THE SAN JUANS

A complete history of maritime disasters in the San Juan Islands, from the earliest schooners to the naval aircraft of World War II.

MYSTERIOUS SAN JUAN ISLAND

A collection of strange accounts and bizarre history from the famed "Pig War island," including UFO encounters, sasquatch sightings, ghosts, and everything in-between.

Contents

When you have eliminated the impossible, whatever remains, however improbable, must be the truth.

SIR ARTHUR CONAN DOYLE

Though in many of its aspects this visible world seems formed in love, the invisible spheres were formed in fright.

HERMAN MELVILLE

For we wrestle not against flesh and blood, but against principalities, against powers, against the rulers of the darkness of this world, against spiritual wickedness in high places.

EPHESIANS 6:12

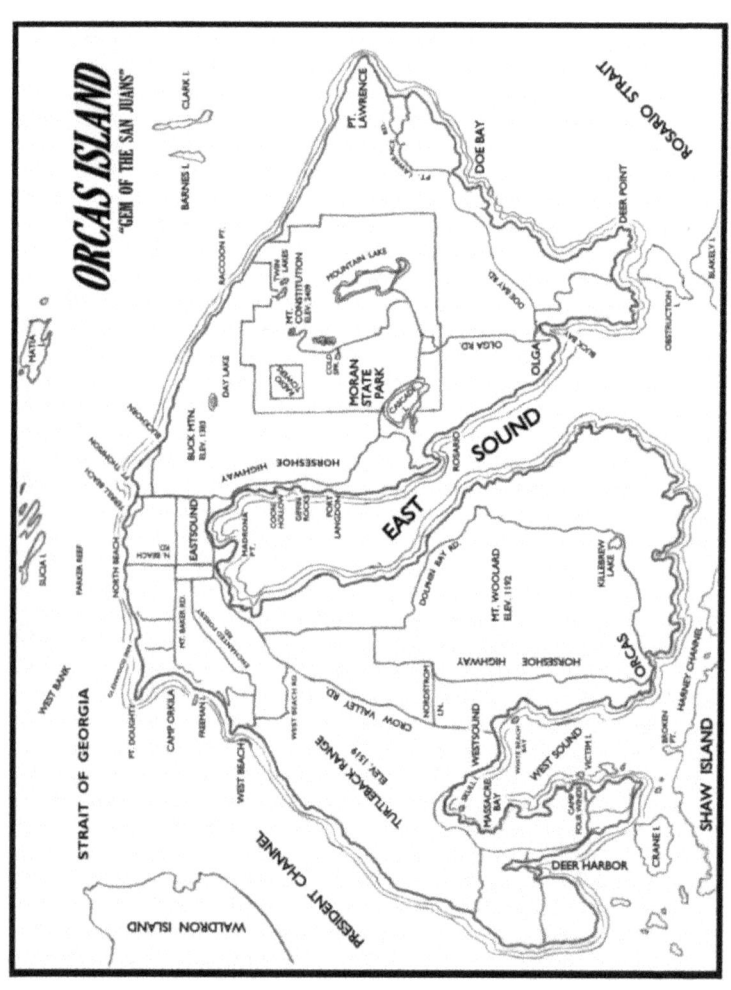

Introduction

Orcas Island is, indisputably, one of the more storied and picturesque locations in the lower forty-eight. The largest of the San Juan Islands, and the highest among the peaks of a drowned mountain range, Orcas sits centrally located in the sound region, with unparalleled views of the Olympics, Cascades, and Pacific Ranges. With its fertile soil and "banana belt" climate, the island has attracted settlers since the first Paleo-Indians wandered down from the wild Alaskan land bridge, earning appellations such as "Ultima Thule," "the Jersey of Puget Sound," or "the Gem of the San Juans."

Orcas itself boasts breathtaking vistas, ancient forests, and charming villages, but that is hardly all: there are other, more intriguing attractions that lie off the beaten path. Overgrown trails lead to washed-out lime pits and forgotten places, while elsewhere, behind the dark windows of old island homes, strange things move in the shadows and go bump in the night. The island, so sunwashed and vibrant during the spring and summertime, has a dark aspect that creeps in when the sky turns overcast and the leaves are carried off by the wind.

My first exposure to the odd-side of island life was at the summer bonfires sometimes held at North Beach. A certain old-timer named Frank Worden*, since passed on, would delight in telling about the old days when the elk and beaver still ruled the land, and when the sandhill cranes held "war dances" on Crescent Beach—and then, sometimes, he would tell the *other* stories. His voice rose and fell like waves on the beach as he regaled the spellbound listeners with tales of lost treasures, haunted houses and the terrible "Little People" . . . stories that one would have been hard-pressed to find in any history books.

Unusual Orcas Island was written so that you, the reader, might have some semblance of the experience I did first hearing Worden's yarns all those years ago. It won't be quite the same, but it's as close as I can manage.

The sources for this book are numerous, ranging from first-hand accounts to newspaper clippings, and everything in-between. I have used real names when possible, but in cases where the interviewee wished to remain anonymous, I have added asterisks (*) to den-

ote the pseudonym.

This book, while nominally nonfiction, should not be interpreted as pure fact; there are details here that can likely never be corroborated. However, as a glimpse into a fog-shrouded past inhabited by settlers and Indians, ghosts and other things, it may prove a valuable insight. The veil between past and present is quite thin on Orcas Island, and if you can suspend your disbelief in the supernatural for just a little while, you may find yourself both shuddering at the spookiness of it all, and connecting with Orcas Island's engrossing history.

Echoes of an Old Murder

It was in the February of 1902 that Tom Robertson gunned down Jack Hand on the Olga road. It was an incident that shook the tight-knit island community to its core, and would become the subject of hushed and tantalizing conversation for generations to come; and it would give rise to a multitude of bone-chilling tales.

Robertson and Hand were both early settlers of the Olga area, being among those first moccasined ramblers who paddled ashore and built their cabins along the remote island coves. Robertson was born in Maryland, and had come west as a young boy in 1851—Hand's history has been more difficult to establish. By 1902, both men had settled into more genteel lifestyles, as the population grew and Olga became a regular stop for steamers like the *Buckeye* and the *Lydia Thompson*. Robertson by then had a wife and children, and the seventy-seven-year-old Hand lived alone on a stump ranch owned by the county treasurer, adjoining the Robertson farm.

The feud supposedly arose from an incident some twenty years before, when Robertson had borrowed three hundred fence rails from Hand, with the promise of an equal number of replacements. Hand maintained that he had never received the rails back, and Robertson called the old man a liar. This dispute, coupled with both men's alcoholism, festered for the two decades leading up to the shooting, with Robertson making it clear to Hand that he was "not to speak to any of [his] children."

February 17th, 1902, started out as a day like any other; it was relatively clear that morning, and Jack Hand decided to make the two-mile journey into Olga, accompanied by Larkin Savage, with a wagon-load of poultry and produce. Upon delivering his load to Anthony Ohlert, he went to Jefferson Moore's general store, where, as it happened, one of the Robertson girls was counting out a basket of eggs she had sold the shopkeeper.

Hand, apparently not sensing any danger, "play-fully put his hands on her shoulders," and the girl "turned and looked at him and laughed," according to the *San Juan Islander* of February 20th. What the old man failed to realize, however, was that the girl's father had been sitting unseen by the stove, and when the girl left, Robertson stood and confronted Hand. A vicious tirade ensued, and Hand left the store only after Moore and a man named Theodore Morrow intervened. All that morning, Robertson had been nursing a handle of whiskey he had picked up from the steamer *Buckeye*—whiskey was widely known to inflame Robertson's "passions"—and he was now as ill-tempered as ever.

Hand had escaped the confrontation mostly uns-cathed, but later in the afternoon, with the sun low in the sky, he would make the fateful decision to return to Olga, to purchase a sack of nails from Ohlert's store. He visited with Ohlert for a time and imbibed in liquor himself before leaving.

At around five o'clock, returning on foot with the sack slung over his shoulder, Hand was set upon by Robertson on the road outside the Moore place, about a mile from town. This time, Robertson was armed with a massive .45-90 Winchester rifle. Fifteen -year-old Ella Moore, who witnessed the events from the front window, testified that Robertson had arrived at the Moore place several minutes before Hand, and that he and Hand had had a largely unintelligible exchange that resulted in Hand exclaiming, "Oh Tom, you wouldn't do anything like that!"

The two proceeded to struggle, with Robertson raining blows on the feeble Hand, who was even-tually able to throw a rock at his attacker—the crux of Robertson's "self-defense" story. The rifle was fired inadvertently, sending a round straight through the front of the Moore house, and Hand managed to limp away. Robertson fired again, and Hand lay dead, shot in the back, the road strewn with nails.

Robertson, undoubtedly sobered, soon went to Olga and turned himself in to the Justice of the Peace, Jack Snowden. Since there were no available deputies on the island, Snowden charged Ohlert and a man named Bill Emch with delivering Robertson to the sheriff's office in Friday Harbor, which they did later that evening. Robertson maintained that he had acted in self-defense, and even penned a letter to that effect to the *Islander*—notably claiming that Hand had tried to kill him on at least four occasions in the past, and that his whiskey had been for "medicinal purposes." He made no reference to the killing or how he came to be standing at the Moores' front gate with a loaded rifle.

Robertson retained the legal services of Phillips & Peringer, with his chief counsel being Josiah N. Phillips, a prominent Whatcom attorney who had once been a judge in Los Angeles. Robertson was arraigned before Judge George A. Joiner on March 18th and, to no one's surprise, entered a plea of "not guilty."

His trial began on April 22nd, and numerous witnesses would give their testimony, including Ella Moore, whose account was widely regarded as the most important of the trial. The young girl reportedly exhibited a remarkable "poise" that moved many of the jurors.

As for the defense, Robertson's own testimony was called "undoubtedly one of the most dramatic incidents ever witnessed in a court room in this state." The grey-haired Robertson, perched on the witness stand, gave a wild account of his run-in with Hand, his "deep set eyes flashing with excitement and passion" as he recounted the tale. He further elaborated on his background, relating how he had first come to the Pacific coast as a young boy, and revealing that his mother and his brother had both died in the hellish insane asylum at Fort Steilacoom.

Perhaps the strangest testimony of the trial was that of two Whatcom men, H.D. Fish and V.W. Taylor, who had gone on a number of hunting trips with Robertson. Fish and Taylor both stated, under oath, that the accused man had expressed his fear of Hand to them, and, strangest of all, had spoken of "[…] having had a personal encounter with the devil, and also about a haunted island somewhere in the Gulf of Georgia."

Despite the apparent effort to reinforce an insanity plea, the verdict was reached on Saturday, April 26th—guilty of murder in the second degree, with a sentence of fifteen years in the state penitentiary. As the *Islander* decried, with a liberal use of capital letters, "If he conducts himself in the penitentiary as a model prisoner and obtains all the 'good behavior' credits allowed under the penal code he can be a free man in NINE YEARS and FIVE MONTHS." The *Islander* was wrong, however—Robertson was released after only six.

Robertson's post-parole life was largely one of

obscurity, and it seems he returned home to Olga and took up his previous life of farming and horticulture. In 1911, he reported that a quantity of apples and seed potatoes had been stolen out of his barn, but nothing more came of it. One notable item, however, a little A.P. featurette, would run in the back pages of a number of newspapers across the country in February of 1923—almost exactly twenty-one years after the "Olga Tragedy" took place. The article reads:

Believed to be the oldest man to ever enter a state penitentiary in this country, Thomas H. Robertson, aged 90, has started serving his second term in the Washington state penitentiary. Robertson was com- mitted from San Juan County to serve a term ranging from the minimum of six months to the maximum of five years, because he is said to have threatened the life of his 76-year-old son-in-law. His grandson, past 50, interfered, it is said.

The nonagenarian had, in fact, been convicted of second-degree assault. Originally remanded to county custody due to his advanced age, a second sentence by a new judge sent Robertson to the state hoosegow.

"His last episode will probably result in his life ending behind the prison doors," wrote the *Journal*. For once, the papers were prophetic; according to institution records, Tom Robertson passed away at the Walla Walla penitentiary on June 15th, 1925, and was buried in the cemetery there.

ECHOES OF AN OLD MURDER

* * *

Time had its way with the unpleasant tale, and soon enough, to the local children, Tom Robertson became a local legend—the story would be told around a flickering campfire of the "Grey Man," who, fifty years before, had murdered half the town of Olga one-by-one on Halloween night, and who, though bent and wizened, still stalked the woods with a long and rusty scythe, searching for young limbs to carry away in his bloody burlap sack . . .

By the time the "Grey Man" had made his way into the regular rotation around the bonfires at Camp Orkila (see the "Camp Spirit" chapter of this book), the myth had been propelled to even greater heights of lurid and hair-raising fright. The stories now involved the spectral figure of a gruesome and stringy-haired old man who wandered the lonely beaches on foggy days and lurked in the surrounding forest with his "soul-bag"; for he no longer sought his victims' flesh and blood alone. Anyone unfortunate enough to encounter the Grey Man would be found soon after in some remote spot, dead, their hair turned white and their face frozen in a look of sheer terror.

And in Olga, tales were told of phantom gunshots that echoed through the fog on certain evenings, and of strange goings-on along the Doe Bay road. One old tale suggests that Hand's transparent specter can be seen on the road at twilight, still limping toward his doom, while another anecdote, from the 1950s or 60s, recalls that car tires would often go flat outside the old Moore place—the culprit would be a square nail, a type not manufactured since the early 1900s . . .

Why *did* Tom Robertson kill Jack Hand? Was the answer as simple as the prosecution made it seem, a feud over fence rails left to foment? Or were there other currents running just beneath the surface, clear to those involved but now obscured and forgotten? There would be other such quarrels and killings to come in later years, all with an equal number of non-answers. Are such trivial disputes truly to blame for these brutal acts? With a case as old as the Olga Tragedy, we most likely will never know.

Big Footed Islanders

Everyone has heard of the mythical bigfeet; the large, hairy men who inhabit the wild places of North America. But how many associate these legends with Orcas Island? A handful of bigfoot sightings have indeed been reported here over the years, many falling squarely into the category of tall-tale, while others, told by rather reputable sources, may be more plausible than some would care to admit.

One story, most likely falling into the former category, was recounted in a 1941 *Orcas Islander* article. Titled "When Orcas Had a Wild Man," the tale was attributed to a Blaine resident named Cecil Pratt, who had originally come to Orcas as a child in 1894. According to Pratt:

After my folks sold that first homestead to J.L. Gadberry in '01, we lived with the James Armstrongs for a year, and from then on I went to the Tullock [sic] *schoolhouse . . .*

Jim Armstrong was quite the nimrod and could often be found fire-hunting in the orchard. He was also a first-rate raconteur and used to tell us boys stories of his hunts with Ed. Morse and Frank Quinby. A favorite of ours was the story of their run-in with "the wild man" near the upper lake [Author's Note: an old name for Mountain Lake] *some years before.*

A man called "Dutch" Hanck had a band of sheep on the meadows above the lake, and one day he came to Armstrong and asked him to help rid the place of a mountain lion that had carried off two big ewes the night before. Armstrong noted that this lion, or whatever it was, must have been of enormous size, given that it had chosen two fully-grown sheep over the lambs. He enlisted Morse and Quinby, and along with Dutch and his collie called Sultan, they went to look over the pasturage where the sheep had been taken.

They found a blood trail leading down into a draw that was thick with ferns nearly as tall as a man. Of the sheep and their killer there was no sign. It was dusk now, and they lit their coal oil torches and commenced to fire-hunting. With the light of a torch, an animal's eyes will blaze like hot coals, and then it is no trick at all to bring it down. It was no time at all until Sultan got on the trail, and he soon began to growl and bristle at something away up in the tree branches. The men turned their torches to whatever it was, raising their lights higher and higher as they searched for the thing's eyes in the branches above. And soon they found them . . . ten feet in the air, two eyes as big as saucers gleamed red in the torchlight, and the hunters quickly realized that this was not a varmint perched in the branches, but rather a monster of a beast standing as high on its own two feet!

The beast cocked back its head and let out an unearthly howl that shook the men to their core, and with no further prompting they let loose a volley of gun-fire and began their retreat up the draw. The going was slow, however, hemmed up by the tall ferns and the steep country, and soon the beast had gained on the party. As he scrambled up the rocky slope, Armstrong froze as he heard Dutch cry out in terror . . . the thing had snatched him up and was carrying him back into the forest, his screams fading into the night as the beast thundered through the trees and underbrush. The hunters knew they could do nothing for their friend, and paused from their mad clamber to stare off after the awful cries. But they heard another sound as well . . . the furious baying of Sultan, as the brave dog pursued his master and the fiend deep into the woods. Soon there was nothing to be heard at all, and the men continued back to Dutch's camp, where they fortified themselves until daybreak.

With the sun risen, the hunters ventured back into the draw to look for signs of their friend. They followed the trail of destruction where the beast had crashed through the woods, and after a half-mile or so came upon a startling scene . . . there, in a small clearing, was the huge and hairy carcass of the beast, its legs torn to ribbons and dried blood cascading from its mangled throat . . . and next to it was the body of Sultan, a hunk of flesh still clenched between his teeth.

As they took in this strange sight, the men heard a groan from amongst the nearby ferns. It was Dutch, his leg broken and groggy from having been knocked asleep when the wild man dropped him. He said the last thing he recalled, before being dropped, was the beast's howls as Sultan lunged at its legs.

Old Jim Armstrong was a storyteller by nature, and of course the story he told us was a lark, but I will say there was a pearl of truth: after telling it, he'd get up and go over to a trunk and take out something he had wrapped up in oilcloth and say, "And this . . . is the wild man's head!" and then he would make a show of pulling off the cover. It was a skull, quite a lot bigger than a man's, and shaped a lot funnier, too. It had huge eye sockets and a thick brow. You could tell it was very old and had come out of the ground. I've often looked back on it and wondered where it is now. It was just a curio for him, but I would hazard to guess that an institution would like to get their hands on it.

The whereabouts of such a skull, if indeed it ever existed, are unknown today.

* * *

Old-timer Bill McWilliams* claimed that the remains of an unknown hominid had been uncovered on Orcas in the early 1900s; a homesteader had uncovered a skeleton measuring eight feet tall, with "Neanderthal"-like features, buried under a pile of stones near Buck Mountain. The remains were reportedly donated to the local Odd Fellows lodge and used for initiation ceremonies until being lost in a fire in 1950.

Unusual scenes encountered in Moran State Park would also seem to imply the existence of a Gargantuan biped. In the 1890s, a massive boulder was rolled down the side of Mount Constitution and into the orchard of Mr. and Mrs. L.E. Cox, who kept a boarding house at the south end of Cascade Lake. The identity of just who rolled the rock was the subject of much speculation at the time, although the massive size of the stone no doubt caused some to suspect a sasquatch. Much later, in an interview with the author, former camp host Keith Guindon described a number of odd occurrences that took place at Moran during his tenure:

"When I was working at Mountain Lake in about '99 or 2000, I did hear a few things and I saw some things that made me think a little bit. Something pretty bizarre I saw personally was this area near the lake, pretty far off-trail, where all these trees had been ripped up, totally unrooted, and leaned tog-ether in kind of a teepee shape. Now I'm sure the wind could have had something to do with that, but it was only in this one area, about a twenty-foot circle, and some of these trees were kind of far from where they'd been pulled up. So I don't know [...] I read somewhere that people think the sasquatch do that to mark their territory or it's even where they bury their dead.

"I never saw [a bigfoot], but I heard what sounded like a monkey, as crazy as that sounds. Like a chimp-anzee or something, but it was a big, big sound, more like something gorilla-sized or bigger. I heard it from across the lake. And I'd hear the tree knocking everyone talks about, I wouldn't say frequently, but I'd hear it once or twice a week. It would be close to the cabin, too, sometimes. I wouldn't go out at night unless I was packing.

"We'd get campers complaining about all kinds of stuff, too, like there was about a two-week period where people were saying there was a real bad smell at the Primitive Area campground, like a cross between a skunk and a dead body [...] and they were saying they'd hear something big walking through at night, poking around, getting into their coolers and whatnot. Nobody wanted to get out of their tents to see what it was [...] the official line was that it was a bear that swam over, which they do sometimes, but I don't think so, personally.

"I'm still in touch with some of the rangers and the staff over there, and from what I hear this stuff is still going on. But they'll never acknowledge it officially."

Patty Kemp*, who lived on a farm near Doe Bay with her husband Mitchell*, reported finding huge footprints in their muddy field, and heard, on at least three occasions, inhuman, howling screams coming from the woods. Apples and pears would frequently disappear from their small orchard, and the huge tracks lead away into the remote mountain valleys of the state park. Their neighbors had been experiencing similar phenomena for decades, says Patty, although the community consensus was that bears—or possibly homeless individuals—were responsible.

Don Figgs*, who purchased a few acres near Raccoon Point in the 1990s and built a house, stated that he occasionally heard something large crashing through the heavy timber on Buck Mountain, and what sounded like "a guy [...] hitting a big stick on a tree" somewhere in the forest, followed by a similar response from farther away. He also heard someone or something "hoot" once in the late evening, a powerful sound that sent Don's dogs into a frenzy. "It almost sounded like an owl," he said, "or a cross between that and a primate. Whatever it was, it was huge."

Rocks thrown from the treeline would occasionally pelt the house and once landed near Don himself while he worked outside. Don also mentioned that a friend of his had reported similar occurrences while fishing at Twin Lakes—"someone" had heaved an enormous stone into the water several feet away, followed by another that sent the fisherman fleeing.

Whatever the case may be, there can be no doubt that, among vague legends of Orcas Island, the bigfeet lay claim to a prominent place.

Mysterious Mount Constitution

Mount Constitution is the highest elevation in the San Juan Islands, culminating in a windswept peak 2,409-feet above sea level. There is no place quite like it in the world. A narrow road built parallel to a wagon trace from the 19th century winds up to a stone watchtower overlooking what some call the finest sea view in North America. For this reason—and for plenty of others—people have been drawn to Mount Constitution for millennia. As a result, it has become the nucleus for a wide variety of legends.

Named by surveyor Charles Wilkes in 1841 for the famed warship USS *Constitution*, the mountain was originally called *Swelax* in the native tongue. *Swelax* was a holy site for the Swallah tribe, as it was said to be the abode of Raven: a powerful and mysterious figure found in many Coast Salish mythologies. According to one legend, Raven had once feuded with the spirits in Cascade Lake and had cast down a lightning bolt from the mountaintop which killed all the lake's fish. Indeed, no fish could be found in the lake for as long as anyone could remember, until trout and bass were stocked in the early 1900s. The Lummi hero Shalaktst, too, was said to have plunged into the dark waters of Summit Lake, seeking counsel from a spirit who lived there (see the "Blood on the Stone Club" chapter of this book). *Swelax* was regarded as a powerful beacon of *tamanous*, or spiritual energy, in the Coast Salish tradition.

The white man arrived in the 1840s, in the form of Hudson's Bay Company hunters sent to collect hides, meat, and anything else of value. Later influxes would occur in the early 1860s, when prospectors returning from the Cariboo and Fraser River gold rushes passed through the islands and decided to stay on—many early settlers, such as Michael Adams, Charles Shat-tuck, and "Colonel" Enoch May arrived in this manner.

Hushed talk amongst these old-timers of gold ledges and walls of pure Galena ore on Mount Constitution gave way to the announcement that gold-bearing quartz had been found at Newhall—now Rosario—in 1892. A number of islanders and at least two professional outfits staked mineral claims on the mountain and commenced blasting. Plans were drawn up for a tramway that would ferry ore down the

mountainside. In 1897, the area was officially incorp-
orated as the Orcas Island Mining District No. 1.

The mines petered out one by one, and few traces
remained by the time the Civilian Conservation Corps
(C.C.C.) began development of the park in the 1930s.
The shafts and tunnels were gradually choked with
vegetation, and most were dynamited shut by park
rangers in 1985. A notable exception was the Augusta
Mine, which remains open and accessible to this day
(see the "Haunted Mine" chapter of this book).

The shipbuilder and former Seattle mayor Robert
Moran began purchasing the land which now comp-
rises Moran State Park and Rosario in 1905, buying
out the Newhall sawmill and the hardscrabble farmers
living around Cascade and Mountain Lakes. Moran
was soon the owner of nearly five-and-a-half-thou-
sand acres of deserted wilderness, the entirety of
which he donated to the State Parks Committee in
1921.

This newly vacated tract was the subject of an odd
little article in the *San Juan Islander* of June 30th, 1911.
Featured below a piece outlining the plans of San
Francisco financiers to build a cog railway up the
mountain, it read:

*The first engagement in the boundary dispute between the
United States and Great Britain occurred near here last
Sunday night. The light that was showing on the summit of Co-
nstitution every night last week could not be seen on that night.
A detachment of hussars under Capt. A.B.H. Grahame,*

K.C.B., was hurriedly dispatched from Fort Skymalt to the scene. Leftenant [sic] Percy Postlethwaite, who had been left in charge of the light, was not to be found at once, but later in the day some shreds of clothing were discovered. He was undoubtedly eaten up by the big Kodiak bear that escaped from the hotel here last year.

Surprisingly, a bear had indeed been on the loose on Orcas Island—"Higgy," allegedly a cub of that monstrous subspecies found in the Kodiak Archipelago, had been given to the noted writer Ella Rhoads Higginson, a resident of the "Little Bellingham" summer colony in Olga. Higginson, in turn, gave the cub to May Rice, who owned the Olga Inn with her husband Charles, and it was soon the center of attention in the little community. The *Islander* of July 8th, 1910 reported that Higgy had been delivered to Olga aboard the steamer *Burton* and that "[…] the bear is to be set at liberty and a grand bear hunt organized, with E.C. Sterne, of Bellingham, as the master of the hunt." These affluent summer residents, it would seem, were not all-too considerate of their year-round neighbors.

The cub, then weighing only fifty pounds, slipped its collar on October 10th and escaped into the woods. By the following year its reputation had grown in tandem with bear itself—the bruin, now ten-feet tall on his its hind legs and weighing over a thousand pounds, stalked the abandoned homesteads around Mountain Lake and ventured down to Olga and Doe

Bay to steal sheep and ravage the fruit orchards. Deer and sheep carcasses were found eviscerated in the remote draws and glens around Mount Pickett, and Duncan Bower, the game warden, led a hunting party into the hills with middling success.

"Wes Langell is reported to have set a trap for him," declared the *Islander*. "The trap was not large enough to hold him so the bear is wearing it around the jungle for a jewelry ornament."

Lieutenant Percy Postlethwaite seems to be apocryphal, as does the story of his supposed demise; further references to a Canadian or British-operated "light" on Mount Constitution are non-existent. Royal Navy surveyors were known to have made an ascent of the mountain in the early 1860s, where they hoisted a survey balloon and piled a rock cairn that can still be seen today—however, by 1911, the mountain was largely under the ownership of Robert Moran, and the mysterious vanishing of a military officer there would have surely been grounds for more international excitement. This story was almost certainly satire, the deeper connotations of which have been lost to time.

As for the hulking Higgy, who was very much real, the bear met its end at the old Brenaw place, near Olga, in June of 1913. A local man named Sam Lightheart had heard of a recent sighting there and went out to lay for the bruin. When Higgy appeared, Lightheart took aim with his little .22 rifle and dispatched the bear with five well-grouped shots to the head—and thus ended the bloody saga of the

Olga Kodiak, and the possible killer of Lieutenant Postlethwaite.

As an aside: Wes Langell, who'd tried to trap Higgy in 1911, mentioned the bear in a reminiscence article some thirty-three-years later. He referred to Higgy as "a small black bear."

* * *

By the start of the Second World War there was only one piece of private land remaining in the entire park, and it sat squarely on the summit of Mount Constitution. The twenty-three-acre Oldowski homestead, often erroneously called the "Russian Settlement," had been claimed by Polish immigrants Stanislaw and Rosie Oldowski in 1914—and, despite a valiant effort, was never acquired by Robert Moran. Vacated by the Oldowskis in 1926, it was used as a hunting camp until the war, when the military began to establish itself in the park.

In 1941, Orcas Island was a vastly different place. PV-1 Ventura crews out of Ault Field practiced bombing runs on targets such as White Rock and Flattop Island, while the Mount Constitution tower, with its commanding view of the surrounding waterways, was used as an observation and listening post. A forty-four-man detachment of the 2nd Interceptor Command had been transferred to the old C.C.C. barracks at Camp Moran, and a serviceman, equipped with binoculars and a two-way radio, was set up in the wood-paneled room atop the tower with instructions to watch for submarines and enemy aircraft—a cushy alternative, no doubt, to the island battles that raged elsewhere in the Pacific. A year later, the Air Corps men left for Australia, and their installation was turned over to the Coast Guard.

The military presence in the park was lifted following the war, and the communications post on the mountain was ceded to a small Bellingham firm called Mount Constitution Sites. This company erected a series of radio and television towers at the old "Russian Settlement," and later expanded to include broadcasting for federal agencies and others who employ specialized frequencies.

Speculation arose, however, that there were more secretive activities taking place at the remote outpost. The chainlink fencing and former military occupancy spawned rumors of a missile silo or a surveillance station to monitor Soviet submarines in the Strait of Juan de Fuca, and some even surmised that an extremely low frequency (ELF) transmitter was being covertly operated to communicate with the nuclear submarines out of Bangor—or perhaps for even stranger purposes. Such rumors are an apt example of the Cold War paranoia that once gripped the nation.

The site has been quiet ever since, fenced off and surrounded by signs warning of danger from microwave frequencies. The array is isolated from the more "touristy" parts of the mountain, and for most the only indication of its existence has been the red lights of the radio towers that have blinked every night for the past sixty years, a tangible reminder of the island's unusual past.

* * *

The "vibe" that many experience while traveling up the mountain has been called "self-perpetuating," in that the strange feeling is itself caused by tales of strangeness. The feeling was acknowledged as far back as 1912, when an article titled "Some Mysteries of Mt. Constitution" appeared in the *San Juan Islander.*

"The road from Olga to Mt. Constitution is get-ing as famous for strange doings and uncanny sights as it is for nature's real and ideal charms," began the article.

Considering that the road leads through "dry" territory, and that no snakes have been reported seen, one might attribute some of the seeming defects of the eye which sees things which may not be what they seem, to drinking fire-water instead of quenching thirst at the sparkling brook by the roadside. Or possibly, the frequent windings of the road cause dizziness and bogey visions.

The piece further discussed strange and recent happenings on the mountain; an Olga resident had discovered the carcass of a cow tied to a tree near Doc Hilton's old cabin at the summit. No one could explain why someone would lead a cow to such a place, or what became of whoever who led it there.

"Only a few months ago an alarm was sounded and silent prayers ascended for a stranger who went up the mountain for some unknown purpose and was thought to have been lost," said the article, concluding: "The *Islander* cannot deny the truth of these mysterious stories, for the editor saw the man who told them."

Hippies and New Agers believed the island to be a "power spot," sitting over solid quartz and imbued with certain metaphysical qualities beyond the realms of man. Some even claimed that Mount Constitution holds a massive crystal, causing paranormal activity and calling down UFOs from outer space (see the "UFOs and Other Phenomena" chapter of this book).

Devotees of J.Z. Knight and the Ramtha cult, too, contend that the mystical sword of their Lemurian warrior-deity is buried deep within the mountain—itself an emersed remnant of the "lost continent," and a gateway to Agartha and inner-earth. The "Ramth-ites" had swarmed to Orcas beginning in 1986, shortly after Knight had announced that "the end was nigh." The earth had grown tired of human pollution, said Knight, and a cataclysmic "cleansing" was scheduled to occur in May of 1988. Knight had also released a list of "safe places," at the top of which was Orcas—though she also noted that the island would be divided in half by an eighty-foot tidal wave. Ramthites arrived on the future "Orcases" in droves and quickly claimed nearly every available rental property. Their two-year stockpile of food and survival supplies also raised more than a few eye-brows among the leery locals, many of whom feared that Orcas would become the next Rajneeshpuram.

Nevertheless, nothing much came of the strange events; no doubt disappointed by the earth's perseverance, most of the Ramthites had departed the island by 1989. Ramtha's sword, on the other hand, still resides somewhere within Mount Constitution.

Dora Kunz, who co-founded the Theosophist camp on Judd Cove in 1927, maintained that an "angel" lives atop the mountain and curates the island's "therapeutic atmosphere." And at the Polarity Institute, a controversial "healing arts" center once located at Doe Bay, bizarre pseudoscientific research was conducted on "astral energies" and the island's power—though the Polarity people kept their secrets well-guarded.

Tales of inner-earth and subterranean worlds may well derive from the cavern that is, or was, known to exist somewhere along the north end of Mount Constitution. Early mention of the cave is found in an 1890 newspaper article, which detailed its exploration by a group of Seattle men:

[...] *a party of gentlemen left Cascade Bay fully equipped to explore the Orcas Island cave. After traveling a mile inland the party arrived at the entrance of the cave, which is situated on the north side of a large bluff of limestone on Mount Constitution. Candles were now passed around to all the members of the party, who were then ready to begin exploration. We now proceeded under the gulf by crawling on hands and knees for about fifty feet.*

Then the tunnel branched off into four passages three feet high. We went in the main passage for twenty feet. It then opened into a room 11x12 feet, the ceiling being studded with stalactites, which sparkled like diamonds when the light of the candles fell upon them. From this room there were numerous passages leading further under the mountain. We took the largest passage and proceeded, passing through innumerable chambers whose beauty surpassed anything that had ever been seen by any of the party. After proceeding on for some time in the same way, further progress was stopped by a large lake, whose waters were as clear as crystal and as cold as ice. We all gathered on the shore of the lake and drank of its beautiful water. It was now deemed advisable to return to the surface, as our candles were half gone. After reaching the surface a speech was delivered by one of the party, who broke a bottle of champagne, and christened the cave Cascade.

Surprisingly, further mentions of "Cascade Cave" in period sources are few and far between—perhaps the "belly-crawl" entrance was discouraging to those who would otherwise charge admission to such a place. Even the cave's location is difficult to discern— though old-timer Jack Geoghegan left cryptic clues to the effect in a 1930 *Friday Harbor Journal* article, writing:

29

Under the ridge, where the tall trees wave,
*   there is a small hidden cave.*
*   If I was small enough I'd crawl,*
*   Back to its farthest dripping wall.*

Notably, Geoghegan also indicated that the cave was near the old sulphur spring—which is not known to have flowed in recent years, but once existed near the north end of Cascade Lake and Otter's Pond (see the "Haunted Mine and Mysterious Mineralogy" chapter of this book).

Pioneer memoirist James F. Tulloch described his exploration of the cave—or a similar one, at least—at around the same time.

"The cave is a small affair in a limestone ledge on the upper side of the road near the old Harrison place," he wrote. "Jack [Geoghegan]'s brother Jim and I, accompanied by Rev. S.R.S. Gray gave it the once over, at least Jim and I did, but the Reverend backed out claiming a bad heart, 'lack of nerve' we thought it. We crawled in about 60 feet or more when it ended in a crack inclining upward, and too small for further progress."

An answer to the puzzle may well be found in a 1966 geological survey—the author, Wilbert R. Danner, examined an abandoned lime quarry in the general location, writing: "Near the central part of the east face of the quarry a small solution cavity about 2 feet in diameter extends back into the limestone an unknown distance. Local residents report that this lime- stone body contained a small cave before it was quarried."

Still, the cave described by the Seattle explorers is one of considerable depth, and would surely have been noted by Danner—and limestone bluffs, untouched by turn-of-the-century quarrying, still exist on the northern flank of Mount Constitution. It is just as likely that Cascade Cave still exists elsewhere on the mountain, its low entrance overgrown with brush, awaiting rediscovery by some daring and sharp-eyed explorer.

Judging by the surfeit of stories surrounding Mount Constitution, it would be fair to say that this landform has been capturing imaginations for quite some time, and will undoubtedly continue to do so for untold generations to come.

Orcas Island Lakes

Cascade Lake, a longtime favorite of locals and tourists alike, sits in the natural depression between Mount
Constitution, Entrance Mountain and Rosario Hill. At
three-quarters of a mile in length, it is the island's
second largest lake, and with its famed population of
cutthroat, kokanee, and largemouth bass is perhaps
the most celebrated freshwater fishing destination in
the San Juans. Ringed by picturesque trails that wind
down to bluffs, lagoons, and a frayed rope-swing that
sways from *bonsai*-like branches, the lake and its
adjoining campgrounds have attracted sightseers for
well over one hundred years. Why, then, does such an
idyllic place warrant its own chapter in a book of
oddities?

As discussed in the previous chapter, Raven, the

god of the Swallah, had cast down a bolt of lightning that killed the entire fish population of Cascade Lake—a retribution against the shadowy spirits who dwelled there. Today, there are many who believe that these spirits never left—and may be responsible for the many strange stories associated with the area.

A number of drownings have occurred there over the years, including the owner of the Doe Bay store in 1917, a young fisherman in 1932, and a motorist who plunged into the dark waters in 2007. A former defense contractor, too, was found dead of mysterious causes in his tent near the lake's lagoon in 2014. He had been camping off-grid and was badly decomposed, as no one had known of the man's disappearance for months.

Tales of a "lake monster" have also been told occasionally, although there is little to suggest that these stories are anything more than yarns recited around the nearby campfires. One visitor claimed to have encountered a "lake dragon" near the lagoon in 2015, a reptilian creature resembling the roots of a floating log that menaced the visitor's dogs. This storyteller also referenced rumors of subterranean sea tunnels that connect Cascade Lake with the nearby sound, thus allowing access by the infamous sea serpent *Cadborosaurus* (see the "Out of the Depths" chapter of this book). The truth of this tale, of course, has yet to be ascertained.

A more realistic rumor concerns the massive fish said to populate the lake. Thirty-to-forty-pound cutthroat have supposedly been seen, and even larger fish of an unknown species allegedly lurk below the bluffs on the western shore—said by some to be sturgeon, supposedly introduced by the owner of a hotel which had stood at the south end of the lake in the 1890s. The author of this book can attest that something massive nearly ripped the rod out of his hands while fishing off these bluffs in 2013.

Mountain Lake is Cascade's larger, more remote sibling. Sitting roughly five hundred and sixty feet higher and reaching depths of over one hundred feet, it is considered less inviting due to its colder temperature and somber atmosphere. Tales of ghostly "tribal" drums at the lake have circulated for years, as have reports of UFOs and similar activity, such as a bizarre "hum" with no apparent source (see the "UFOs and Other Phenomena" chapter of this book).

Day Lake, lying in the high saddle between Buck Mountain and Mount Constitution, was named for an early homesteader named Oscar Day. Day had entrusted a friend with a sum of money meant to sustain him through his twilight years, but when Day called on this "friend" for the savings, he found that they had been embezzled. Believing he had no other options, Day took his own life in April of 1897. To this day, the forest around Day Lake is said to be haunted by the man's restless spirit, in the form of a ghostly lantern seen bobbing through the trees on dark nights.

Twin Lakes, once known as Crater Lakes for their

surprising depth, are located beyond Mount Constitution's eastern face—and are said by some to contain
abnormally-large salamanders. The "bottomless" lakes
had been homesteaded by Pierre Barnes in the 1890s,
and were a popular respite for men employed at the
isolated Estelle limeworks. Known for their sizable
trout population, as well as the occasional rough-skin-
ned newt or long-toed salamander, one local woman
had a distinctly unusual sighting to report there:

"I was walking my dog over the little bridge [at
Twin Lakes] when she started acting kind of skittish,
and she started growling and staring off into the
bushes ahead of us. My first thought was it might be a
bear, because one had been seen recently, but then I
saw this thing crawl out of the underbrush and cross
the trail, and it went into the water [...] it was probably about four feet long, slimy looking, and it had
kind of a red stripey pattern that reminded me of a
diamondback rattlesnake [...] when I got home the
first thing I did was look it up, and the closest I could
find was a Pacific giant salamander. But the book says
those only grow up to about thirteen inches, and of
course what I saw was much, much bigger."

Frank Worden*, the unofficial "dean" of island
folklore, often told of how the area around Killebrew
Lake, near the Orcas Landing, was haunted by the
evil-eyed spirit of Lars Brown. Brown, a hulking
blacksmith of Danish extraction, was well-known

across the island as a "woman-hater," and according to historian Fred John Splitstone, "[...] the pioneer women of that part of the Island, who were not timid souls by any means, refused to pass his cabin at night unless accompanied."

In 1882, Brown was accused of murdering a Waldron Island man named Yves J'Affret in what would prove to be Orcas Island's first "cause célèbre" murder case.

It seemed that the Frenchman and the Dane had quarreled over money at an Indian camp called "the Rancheria" where local men came to drink. J'Affret, in a drunken stupor, dropped a handful of gold pieces, which Brown was kind enough to collect and return. The Frenchman, however, accused Brown of keeping one of the coins, which the blacksmith angrily denied.

J'Affret appeared at Brown's cabin later that night and began beating on the door, causing a disturbance loud enough to summon the neighbors. The argument soon turned to another subject altogether—Brown accused the married J'Affret of having relations with an Indian girl named Ginny. J'Affret rebuked the charge, and the confrontation ended with Brown physically lifting the Frenchman and tossing him out into the dark.

J'Affret soon returned, however, and Brown said in no uncertain terms that he would shoot to kill if J'Affret attempted entry. "You are a coward, and I will chance it," came the reply. He breached the door and Brown shot J'Affret in the stomach. The ball did little to stop the intoxicated man, and they continued to clash until Brown again heaved J'Affret out the door—and there J'Affret expired, lying on the stoop in a pool of blood.

Brown was arrested and taken before the Justice of the Peace, a man named John N. Fry, who was admittedly unversed in the intricacies of judicial proceedings. Fry assembled a jury of local men and held a strange, unofficial trial for the accused man, where eyewitnesses were barred from testifying because the very fact of their witness of the shooting made them "prejudiced" against the defendant. The jurors, stared down by the menacing Brown, found the blacksmith not guilty.

The slain man's friends and family were deeply perturbed by the odd incidents on Orcas Island, and upon hearing of Brown's acquittal called on the county prosecutor with complaints that Fry's trial had been a farce. Brown was hauled in again, and this time sent to a proper courthouse at Port Townsend, where yet again he was handed a verdict of not guilty. J'Affret was buried on a lonely point of land on Waldron Island overlooking Boundary Pass.

Despite the seeming conclusion, there was still considerable doubt among those directly involved. It was reported that Brown had threatened a neighbor named Samuel Trueworthy only a few days after the shooting, brandishing an axe and assailing the man with a "tirade of epithets," according to the *North-west*

Enterprise.

"It is well you did not offer to touch me," said Brown, when Trueworthy gave no response. "I would have quartered you with this axe."

Moreover, another neighbor reported that Brown had been seen reloading his pistol immediately after his killing of J'Affret, muttering, "It's not unlikely I'll have to shoot some more damned fools that come around here." As the *Enterprise* expounded, in typically lurid fashion, "The ins and outs of this case are too scandalous for publication," describing Brown as "a sickly, soured and though not necessarily a bad [man], a dangerous old character of the islands; his own old private history but little known, or quite un- known to his neighbors around him."

Brown's own testimony, incidentally, painted a much different view of the case—notably, he claimed that J'Affret had been joined by the mysterious Skookum Tom, a feared and furtive figure of the early days. The two had threatened him with a rifle, said Brown, and he had simply defended himself. He made no mention of the Indian girl Ginny, of whom Brown was said to have had an "unnatural" obsession. The witnesses didn't mention Skookum Tom, either.

Brown was later embroiled in another murder case, when a Shaw Island pioneer named Hugh Park approached the notorious Brown with a strange request: he wanted to be killed. Park was a recluse who had been tormented by his neighbors, shifty men who allegedly coveted his exceptionally beautiful

farmstead—as well as the gold coins Park had supposedly buried there. Brown declined, and in early 1885 the strange situation on Shaw finally came to a head.

A young hunter named James Baker (unrelated to Jim Baker from the "Out of the Depths" chapter of this book) went missing after landing at Park's Bay, a place named for its sole inhabitant. Baker was soon reported missing, and when Sheriff John Kelly and his deputies arrived to investigate, they found Park barricaded in his cabin—with Baker's blood-drained body—and armed with a Winchester rifle. Park killed a deputy after a three-day siege, and on February 2nd he shot himself as lawmen set fire to the cabin.

Lars Brown, his dark reputation now beyond dispute, was also one of the chief combatants in a bloody brawl at the Orcas schoolhouse. A fight broke out during a meeting to discuss the creation of a new school district, and Brown took the limb of a fir tree and beat a man named Charles Martin into an unrecognizable pulp. The fracas only ended after the mediator, school superintendent Ethan Allen, fired his pistol into the ceiling. Brown declared, "Others can shoot, too," and stormed off to retrieve his own firearm. The schoolhouse was empty upon his return.

Martin, incidentally, would die in a manner eerily similar to Hugh Park's in May of 1936, long after Brown's death—Martin's home was engulfed in flames, and the old man's body was found inside, lying over his rifle, "[...] in such a position as to indicate suicide," according to the *Friday Harbor Journal*.

Years after Brown's death, said Frank Worden, the land he had once called home was haunted by his monstrous specter. Women, in particular, were to be wary of the "woman-hating" spirit, described by Worden as seven feet tall and horribly scarred about the face, who wandered the misty shores of Killebrew Lake wielding a massive tree branch and gave chase to interlopers. In Worden's tale, anyone caught by Lars Brown's specter would never be seen again.

Decades later, in the 1980s, a woman shot her husband with a high-powered rifle at their Eastman Road home, wrapped the body in plastic sheeting, and buried him just three feet from the house—and then tossed the murder weapon into Killebrew Lake. It was a strange, and hopefully final chapter of a particularly bloody history.

The lakes of Orcas Island are places of undeniable magic—at least those lakes where the water is warm and clean and inviting to swimmers. And so it is only fitting that this chapter should end on a more pleasant, though unusual, note.

Ben Kunkler had once owned a hotel called the Lake View at the southwestern end of Cascade Lake, where he lived with his big Newfoundland dog Rover. In 1892, Kunkler purchased a small travel magazine and sold the hotel to Mr. and Mrs. L.E. Cox; he then moved to Seattle, and naturally took Rover with.

The dog apparently felt stifled by the cramped and airless city life, however, and one morning was nowhere to be found. It was not until a few days later that the mystery was solved.

Old Rover, it seemed, had wandered down to the Seattle docks and boarded a steamer bound for Fairhaven. When the steamer arrived, Rover made the connection to the *Dispatch*, which he had often traveled on with Kunkler, and had soon enough returned to Olga—where he cheerfully disembarked and made a beeline for his old Cascade Lake home!

Whether visiting the shores of Cascade, Mountain, Day, Twin Lakes, or Killebrew Lake, one can undeniably feel "something" . . . whether that something is simply the tangible beauty of these places, or another kind of power altogether, is left for the individual to decide.

Haunted Hotels

Having been a tourist haven since the late 19th century, Orcas is naturally host to a fair number of hotels—and a few guests who have refused to check out. Hotels such as the Outlook Inn, the Orcas Hotel, and Rosario have long been regarded as "haunted," and it is little wonder why, when one considers the amount history that these rooms have borne witness to over the last one hundred years.

The Outlook Inn, one of the oldest buildings in Eastsound, began life as a general store erected by Charles Shattuck in the late 1850s. Slowly expanded over time, the structure was remodeled into its present form by the Sutherland family in 1891 and named the East Sound House. The Inn would change hands a number of times during the next few decades, under names such as the Beach Hotel and the Mount Constitution Inn, before finally being christened the "Outlook" by Fred P. Meyer in the 1940s.

A mysterious individual named Louis Gittner arrived on Orcas in 1964. A noted Hollywood mystic, self-help author, and New Age "prophet," Gittner was drawn to the area by rumors of heavy UFO activity and a "vortex" off Indian Island. By 1968, Gittner had purchased the Outlook Inn under the auspices of the "Louis Foundation," feeling that the Outlook, with its commanding view of East Sound and the vortex, was a deeply spiritual place.

Devotees of Gittner and others seeking New Age enlightenment soon flocked to the Inn, and dark rumors of drug abuse and occultism began to swirl about the place. Most God-fearing islanders were deeply suspicious of this new long-haired element and their perceived hijacking of an island institution—fears that were confirmed when, one Sunday, members of the commune paraded across Main Street fully nude to bathe in the spiritually-charged waters . . . in full view of the Episcopal congregation.

Rumors of witchcraft and mind control abounded during this period, especially as public perception of the "Summer of Love" began to sour, and as the drug -addled, occultish underbelly of the hippie movement made headlines with Charles Manson and the Haight-Ashbury milieu. The Outlook Inn, though in reality a peaceful commune, became fodder for all-manner of bizarre and scandalous talk. Some tin-foil islanders even suggested later that the Louis Foundation was a front for the CIA and their fabled psychedelic drug experiments. These rumors, of course, were completely unfounded.

"For a century, a few salty settlers and soul seekers have lived here in rough ideological balance," wrote Peter Waldman of the *Wall Street Journal*. "But in recent years, an influx of free spirits from the mainland, touting such services as channeling, breathing awareness and group midwifery, has tipped the scales."

"Their ultimate goal is to do away with anybody who believes there's such a thing as evil," said longtime resident Barbara Russell.

By the late 1980s, however, the Outlook had shifted its business model—or rather, created one—and begun catering to a more "normal" clientele. The new owners made significant improvements to the property and erased much of the Inn's ramshackle New Age character; the only real remnant being the rustic "Chapel of Light" by the back pond. Still, it is only natural that a place as spiritual as the Outlook Inn should claim its fair share of ghostly goings-on:

"There's a ghost we called 'the Major,' because he was a Confederate soldier in the Civil War," said a former employee named Jason Lynaugh. "We had a maid named Cindy* and there were days she wouldn't clean one of the rooms, because she'd say the Major was in there and he didn't like to be disturbed."

Lynaugh likely refers to Major Edmund Clare

Fitzhugh, scion of an old Virginia family, who had been tapped by a San Francisco syndicate to establish and manage the Sehome coal mine at Bellingham Bay in the early 1850s. He accumulated power quickly through his family connections and soon held a multitude of prominent positions, including Democratic Party chairman, Indian agent, and military aide to the governor.

Fitzhugh would also wed Xwelas, sister of Chief Sehome, which served to further his influence with the local tribes. One of Fitzhugh's sons by Xwelas, Mason, would later become embroiled in a famous murder case on Orcas, when Xwelas gunned down her third husband at the Langdon Lime Works (see the "Kilns" chapter of this book).

Fitzhugh was himself accused of murder: in 1857, he killed a man named Wilson who was allegedly trespassing in his back garden—though many believed it was, in fact, a cold-blooded murder over a woman. Despite this, Fitzhugh would be appointed to the Territorial Supreme Court the following year, allowing him to effectively absolve himself of the accusations. Five years later, he would abandon Xwelas and his two sons and return east, where he was commissioned in the Confederate Army on the staff of his old friend, General George Pickett—a key player in the 1859 Pig War, and the namesake of Orcas Island's UFO-haunted Mount Pickett.

Fitzhugh is said to have stayed at Charles Shattuck's place for a period during the early 1860s, perhaps in the course of dealings with "Colonel" Enoch May—a mutual associate of his and Shattuck's. May was a shadowy figure of the early days, a gambler who had drifted south from the played-out Cariboo mines and settled near Eastsound. A smuggler, confidence man, political boss, and "procurer" of Indian wives for the local white bachelors, May was to Orcas and the San Juans as Fitzhugh was to Whatcom. Though Shattuck's original structure is enclosed within the current Inn and changed beyond recognition, it is Fitzhugh's ghost that allegedly haunts the Outlook today.

"I felt the Major plenty of times but I only saw him once," continued Lynaugh.

"I was messing around with the fusebox and Cindy came up to me and said she had to go into [the room] even though she could feel the Major wasn't having it. I guess all the rooms were booked except that one and there was going to be a guest checking in soon. So I went in there with her while she cleaned, just to keep an eye on things, and pretty soon I start to feel something. The hairs on my neck were standing up and Cindy was feeling it too. But she kept making the bed. So I start looking around because I'm kind of nervous, and that's when I saw him. There was a big full-length mirror and I saw a glimpse of this guy with a beard and old-fashioned clothes standing there in the reflection. Then all the lights in the room flickered, and I said 'hey, it's time to go.' The

Major didn't want to be disturbed."

Another employee, Kara Barnhart*, discussed a personal experience that left her deeply shaken. It was the dead of winter in 2005 and a nor'easter was raging across the islands. Kara was manning the front desk that night, and was already sufficiently unsettled by the wind that shook the old building and rattled the window panes . . . a situation made worse by the fact that there was only one guest in the entire building.

"It was probably around eleven thirty or midnight," says Kara, "and I was just sitting at the desk reading a book. The lights had been flickering all that night because of the storm, and then finally the power went out. So I lit a kerosene lamp while I waited for our maintenance guy to come and start the generator."

The maintenance man was taking his time, however, and all Kara could do was sit and read as the lamplight cast eerie shadows on the walls. Only a few minutes had passed before Kara realized that she wasn't alone.

"I was in kind of a bubble of light," says Kara, "and I couldn't really see anything outside of it. But I kept seeing something out of the corner of my eye [...] and finally I saw her. I saw a woman, just for a brief second, standing at the edge of the light. She was wearing an old-fashioned dress and she was staring right at me. And then the lamp flickered, and she was gone."

The staff has taken to calling the spirit "Millie," though some believe it is a former owner named Blanche Irene Baker. Guests have reported similarly disturbing incidents, such as "someone" running up and down the deserted upstairs hallways, and knocking coming from inside empty rooms.

There are those, too, who believe that this odd activity may be connected to an "ancient Indian burial ground." This theory is at least partly plausible; in 1999, road workers *did* unearth an ancient skeleton outside the Outlook. Crews had been installing curbs and parking areas along Main Street when they found the bones.

"We had to stop the work order immediately after finding it," said Dan Kimple of Island Excavating. "We were all there when it was found […] it's not fun to disturb a person's eternal resting place."

Archaeologists determined that the remains were that of a Lummi woman who had died hundreds—if not thousands—of years before. The tribal council debated for days on whether or not to reinter the remains; eventually, a Lummi representative visited the site and decided that the woman would remain where she lay. The road crew placed a steel plate over the grave and sealed it with concrete. The roadwork continued, and today the woman rests beneath the small parking area across from the Inn.

The vortex, meanwhile, supposedly just south of Indian Island, continues to exert its strange influence over Eastsound and the Outlook Inn. The impetus for Gittner's purchase of the Inn, the vortex is said to cause strange and vivid dreams among guests—and, stranger still, is said to function as a cosmic fueling station for otherworldly craft to "charge their batteries," as Louis Foundation higher-up Starr Farish stated in a CBS interview.

Gittner's followers believed Orcas to be a remnant of the lost continent of Atlantis, a scientifically and spiritually-advanced society that had mastered the arts of antigravity and crystal-power. According to Gittner's followers, UFOs could be seen gliding over the Inn and the little island and diving into sound, to avail themselves of the ancient Atlantean vortex that causes harbor seals to swim trance-like in a perfect circle, as one islander reported.

"I can't tell you how many times people come into our little inn, and they say, 'wow, it feels like I'm home, it feels like I've arrived, it feels like I belong here,' and I think that it has to do with that they actually lived, in one form or another, on this continent at one time in the past," said Farish.

No matter how one feels as to the veracity of these mystic tales, one fact that cannot be denied is that a magnetic disturbance *does* exist in the area of the purported vortex—just south of Indian Island, in a spot marked "Local Magnetic Disturbance" on several hydrographic charts, compass needles deflect bizarrely and boaters are left to navigate by sight, the sun, and the stars.

* * *

Perched on a hill above the Orcas Landing, the iconic Orcas Hotel has been serving guests since 1904, and, like its contemporaries, has a rather colorful past. It was operated by the Van Moorhem family for over forty years—and some would say they never really left. The ghost of proprietress Octavia van Moorhem is said to pace the upstairs hallway at odd hours and, occasionally, send kitchenware flying off the shelves, while on the porch a man is heard screaming and phantom streaks of blood appear and disappear in a flash—perhaps the residuals of a shootout that occurred there between lawmen and a fugitive bank robber in 1913.

In 2017 the hotel was visited by a "professional ghost hunter" named Randall Maier, of the group Bellingham Paranormal Investigations. Staying in Room 9, the "Blind Bay" suite, he and his partner set up their equipment and settled in for the night—and what they would claim to experience is truly spine-tingling.

"The first thing we did was turn on the EVP recorder [...] that stands for electronic voice phenomena, which in layman's terms is basically a spirit trying to make contact through audio," said Maier.

"I started walking around the room asking, 'is there anyone here who'd like to make contact?' while my partner was filming with the IR camcorder. We played it back and there was nothing intelligible at first, then there was what sounded like someone breathing heavily for a few seconds. And then we both heard a very audible voice say 'can I come in?' At that point I asked for the spirit's name, and—you can debate with my partner about this, because it's not the clearest, but it sounds to me like it says 'Cornelius.' Now, we'd been expecting to contact the spirit of Octavia van Moorhem, since we were told she's the most active in the hotel, but this was a man, apparently [...] we checked the recording in a couple hours and we heard more breathing, some mumbling, and a voice that said 'no, no, no' over and over again for a few seconds.

"The next night we did some recording in the hall, and we picked up a shadow on the camcorder. There was a voice that said 'the end' and we heard some thuds and thrashing sounds coming from one of the rooms that wasn't audible without the recorder. Later on [...] we moved downstairs and recorded in the lobby [...] we picked up a very audible screaming, a man screaming, and a dragging sound. That's in line with a story we were told that people have seen an apparition of a man dragging himself through the front door, covered in blood. There wasn't really anything after that [...] there's definitely a lot of activity there."

The Rosario Resort and Spa is also suitably haunted. Sitting at the tip of Rosario Point, on Cascade

Bay, this grand estate was once the home of Robert Moran, whose legacy is, to say the least, omnipresent on Orcas Island. The fifty-four-room Craftsman-style mansion was completed in 1909 and was a model of modern self-sufficiency; many of the building materials were fashioned on-site, and power was supplied by a private hydroelectric plant. Its views were so majestic that Moran refused to hang pictures on the walls.

He eventually grew weary of the palatial manor, however, and sold the property to California industrialist Donald L. Rheem in 1938. Rheem, of Rheem Manufacturing Company fame, was a resident of Moraga, California, but frequently vacationed at Rosario with his wife, Alice.

Alice Goodfellow Rheem was allegedly something of a "loose woman," a flapper prone to drink and Great Gatsby-esque revelry who inevitably caused embarrassment for Donald—behavior that eventually led to her "banishment" at the isolated estate. During this period, spanning from the 1930s to her death in 1956, islanders recalled Alice frequenting the tavern in Eastsound, arriving astride a Harley-Davidson motorcycle, or sometimes, chauffeured, in her sleek Packard—and almost always dressed in little more than a red nightgown or negligee. She would play cards with the local boys, and could reportedly drink many of them under the table.

The mansion, meanwhile, deteriorated somewhat in her husband's absence, and the road and once-celebrated gardens became badly overgrown with blackberry and wild rose. Alice was seen wandering the property alone, wearing her signature red gown and usually with a mixed drink in her hand. Eventually stricken with health problems, she returned to the Bay Area, where she passed away at the age of fifty-four.

In the years since, tales have been told of the phantom "Lady in Red," purportedly Alice Rheem, who is often sighted performing ghostly activities in a red gown. Islanders have long reported a scarlet-clad spirit barreling down the road near Rosario on a Harley-Davidson motorcycle, and even once in the mansion itself—though activity of a less dramatic sort is more commonly encountered.

Disembodied, high-heeled footsteps are often heard in the second and third-floor hallways, and many feel a presence in "the Boardroom," a large suite that was once Alice Rheem's bedroom.

"This is the room [where] people who have sort of sensitive, paranormal experiences feel her," said general manager Christopher Peacock, in the 2016 documentary *The Ghost in Red*. "The hair on the back of their neck stands up and they often say, 'this is the room where she is most of the time'."

Peacock went on to discuss a ghost hunting team's spine-tingling experience in the Boardroom some years back:

"We had a paranormal group here doing research one Halloween night [...] one of the things they had was a night-vision camera, which had picked up an orb floating around this room. The other thing they had was a recording device, [and] at about three in the morning, they heard a party . . . and it was like there was a full bar downstairs for about ten seconds, with people talking and laughing . . ."

Guests have also reported sounds of a more scandalous nature, including a man and a woman "giggling" and heels clicking together—naturally, with no apparent source. A pair of incidents in 1987 were particularly noteworthy. A young housekeeper had decided to spend the night after a long day and found herself billeted in Alice Rheem's old bedroom—a room not usually rented out. The girl was only settled in for a few minutes before she sensed "something" in the room, and thought she saw a shadow . . . and then she felt the cool touch of phantom fingers running down her hand. Terrified, she dressed quickly and fled—but not before returning the key to the front desk, just before midnight.

The next morning, a trio of traveling entertainers appeared at the front desk looking unusually haggard, and informed the clerk that they had been kept awake all night by the sounds in the next room—the room that had been the housekeeper's.

"But that's impossible," said the clerk, glancing up at the key on the board. "The room was empty after midnight."

More strange goings-on were chronicled by a

guest in 2007. After a late-evening dinner, the woman and her husband had wandered up to the deserted second floor, where several rooms are open as a self-guided museum.

We had only been up there for about 5 minutes when my husband and I split up. He went into one room, while I went into another. We had no prior knowledge of any unusual history. Upon entering this bedroom, I instantly realized I was not alone. The feeling I had at the time is hard to describe —other than to say that the hair on the back of my neck and arms stood straight up and I distinctly felt the presence of someone in the room with me. I turned around but no one was there. However, the feeling to leave that space was overwhelming me!

Another guest, in the late 1990s, encountered a ghost on the grand staircase at around one in the morning, and soon after saw "ghostly figures" beyond the lamplit parking lot.

The Roundhouse, an odd, circular little structure of whitewashed concrete on a lonely bluff beyond the mansion, was constructed by Robert Moran as a playhouse for his two younger children.

"It is all concrete, even the roof," wrote Glen Porter, one of the builders employed by Moran, who later opened Porter's Garage in Eastsound.

"It is a true circle and contains three rooms, each one of them equipped for baking, a second one is a kitchen and the third a sitting room. Here Mrs. Moran and Nellie [Moran's daughter] did canning and preserving, made candies and fancy cakes and such things away from the kitchen in the mansion that was a busy place since it had to provide meals for a large family and lots of hired help."

The Roundhouse, modern and almost resembling some weird craft descended from the heavens, was eventually converted into a luxury suite by the resort owners, and is today Rosario's premiere accommodation.

"It was a beautiful room, but full of spiders," said Renee Hoagland, who rented the Roundhouse with her family in 2011. "My son, who was seven years old at the time, knew something was different right away. As soon as he walked through the door, he turned to me and said, 'mom, there are ghosts here'."

Renee had a number of odd encounters to report.

"We stayed there for three nights, and on the first, I woke up in middle of the night because the TV had been turned on. My husband slept right through it and I turned it off. Later I woke up again, because I heard someone walking around right outside. Walking around and around the [building].

"The second night was a little more off- putting. I woke up and I saw someone walking back and forth in our room. I was half-asleep and thought it was our son, so I went back to sleep. I asked our son the next morning if he had been in our room pacing last night, and he said no. The more I thought about it, the more I realized that the figure I'd seen was much taller than a seven-year-old. He'd been sleeping in the other room, on a nice bed the staff had given us.

"A few things happened on the last night, as [my husband] can tell you. The TV turned on again, twice, actually, and my son ran into the room at three or four in the morning saying that a little girl had been crying in the corner for the past hour, and that she'd finally run outside, going straight through the solid door . . ."

Employees, however, are still the likeliest to encounter weird phenomena at Rosario, as the manager himself attested: "As long as I've worked here, which has been thirty-five years, it's employees that tend to see [ghosts]—in fact, so intensely, that two employees left without ever coming back."

One former staff-member, Erin Hebel, shared a few odd encounters from her time as a waitress there in 2009-2010:

"I mostly heard stories from my coworkers, but I did see a ghost my last summer working there in 2010. My shift was over and I was leaving at about nine forty-five or ten, because some people had taken forever eating, and I was walking back to my car when I felt this cold breeze, which shouldn't have been because it was the middle of summer. Then I saw, just ahead of me under a streetlight, was a shadow person. It was the outline of a person but it was completely black, almost like a void. It was there for a second and then it was gone, but it didn't disappear, it kind of like zoomed away.

"The story I was told of why it's haunted was that the owner's wife killed herself in the Music Room in the 50s. She was a little wild for back in the day and her husband didn't like that, so he basically kept her prisoner while he was away on business trips. One day she couldn't take it anymore, so she jumped off the balcony.

"One girl I worked with used to tell me all kinds of stuff about what she'd seen or what people working there had seen. I guess back in the 90s the owners hired a lady who was a professional psychic or a medium, because the resort was going to do a séance on Halloween night, as a special dinner party kind of thing. Apparently when she showed up, she almost fainted coming through the door, because I guess the energy was so strong. She said there were a lot of dead people in there. But she ended up doing the séance anyway, and I guess the whole thing went wrong, because people started getting sick and stuff started moving around, the candles went out [...] anyway, I guess the psychic ended up having to be carried out because she was [...] catatonic.

"The seeing-eye dog thing happened a couple of years before I worked there. Basically, this blind guy checked in, and then that night some staff found him walking towards the water, with just a leash in his hand—the seeing-eye dog was back in his room, but something had been leading him and he'd thought it was the dog.

"I don't work there anymore, thankfully. It's a

beautiful place, but I'm still convinced it was haunted and nothing will change my mind."

At the north end of the island, Smuggler's Villa Resort is supposedly haunted by the apparition of an old Indian woman seen walking the beach, and ghostly lights have been reported flashing out at sea on certain stormy nights—harkening back to the *Prelude* tragedy of 1952 (see the "Ghost Ship" chapter of this book).

The Kangaroo House, just down the road, is allegedly home to an inhuman spirit, in that the eponymous creature can still be heard hopping down the second-floor hallway at odd hours. A previous owner, sea captain Harold Ferris, had brought home a wallaby named Josie from one of his voyages in the 1930s.

Cabin No. 10 at West Beach Resort is said to be haunted by a violent poltergeist that enjoys interrupting a good night's sleep. One guest left a detailed description of the experience in a review from 2009:

On the first night we heard fists pounding on the closed bedroom doors and shuffling of footsteps in the bedroom in our cabin. The next night was far worse. From the hours of 10 a.m. to 4 a.m. there were non- stop frantic pacing footsteps across the deck, in the room and on the roof. There was also a myriad of green flashes of light darting through the room and the total presence of someone in the cabin.

We confronted the resort staff about paranormal activity

and they asked "are you staying in cabin 10?" and we acknowledged we were. They said that a man and his son had died elsewhere and their ashes had been scattered near the beach and since then they have had other reports of weird phenomenon in that cabin.

A staff-member was quick to remind the reviewer that a winter storm had given the island a good thrashing the night of the reported encounter—and that fallen tree branches had later been removed from the roof of the cabin.

"In hindsight, perhaps we shouldn't have played along," said the manager.

West Beach was the site of a small native village called *Xoxolos* that was wiped out by a Haida raid in the late 18th century. Early settler Luther Kimple recalled how an ancient Lummi man had landed at the beach one day and, weeping, declared, "Here I was born." The old gentleman told Kimple of escaping into the woods with his mother when the Haida came, and of afterwards stealing across the straits to Vancouver Island. None of the villagers were left alive. Could this supposed poltergeist be a remnant of the horrors that took place there in the distant past?

All in all, it would seem that, when staying at one of the old hotels on Orcas Island, guests can expect either a restful and rejuvenating night's sleep—or something that is entirely more spine-tingling.

The Haunted Mine and Mysterious Mineralogy

The old Augusta Mine on Mount Constitution sits just off the Cold Springs trail, one of the last physical reminders of the island's gold and silver-fever days of the 1890s. It consists of an adit extending roughly one-hundred-and-forty-feet into the mountainside, and a drift that branches off and crosscuts east to a large stope, where a shaft plunges down thirty feet following a played-out vein. The tunnel was driven by an outfit called the Sunset Gold Mining Company in 1898, whose part-owner and manager, W.E. Markham, claimed to have extracted three hundred tons of ore in 1899 alone. Ore taken from a paystreak in this drift assayed out to fifty-one dollars in gold and three in silver.

Later, several "enterprising islanders" would file for mineral claims on the land purchased by Robert Moran in the early 1900s—a form of squatting that forced Moran to either take legal action or to buy out the claimants for exorbitant prices. Still, many would later speculate that the gold rumors *had* played a role in Robert Moran's decision to buy up the entirety of the Orcas Island Mining District—from the Newhall brothers' first strike at Cascade Bay, to the L.E. Cox mine near Cascade Lake—and higher up the mountainside, the Ohlert brothers' tunnel at Mountain Lake, and the Greenhorn and Augusta operations, among others. Surely, these islanders said, there must be some promising ore left untouched in the new park.

Stories have circulated for years that a lower level of the Augusta had collapsed during the mine's heyday and that a dozen miners were subsequently entombed, although there is no period evidence of any kind to support this claim. The legend persists, however, and was discussed in a 1941 *Orcas Islander* article of uncertain authorship:

The old Markham mine on Mt. Constitution that many of our youngsters are no doubt intimate with has long been the subject of a "campfire tale" which suggests that a dozen Chinamen were buried alive there many moons ago. With this article I hope to set the record straight: no such tragedy ever occurred . . . that was recorded. You see, it seems that any historical "fact" that isn't immediately written down in the local rag will eventually be relegated to "fancy"—that is, only a legend. The fact is, no cave-in was reported while the mine was active and so . . . it never happened. But in conversation with Mr. Walter Dykeman, I was told otherwise.

Mr. Dykeman, a resident of Orcas these past 57 years, informed me that such a disaster had taken place. Says Dykeman: "I remember it well. Three or four coolies were down the shaft when a small tremor struck. The mine is built along a fault-line and so the tunnel collapsed." More luridly: "They were sealed alive down there for a few days, and you could hear them tapping. But eventually the tapping stopped."

Is this another case of historical satire, or could the old mine really hold such a dark secret? The answer may very well be yes, if the paranormal activity reported there is any indication. Zak Perdomo, another "paranormal investigator," claims to have experienced some of this eerie phenomenon first-hand:

"I went up there two years ago to shoot a video for my YouTube channel, since a friend of mine had told me I needed to check it out, and [...] I felt uneasy right away. This tunnel had serious enough energy that I wasn't sure if I wanted to keep going, but I said screw it, you know. I was recording for EVPs and filming with my full-spectrum camera the whole time. I got to the side tunnel and immediately I felt like there was something at the other end that was watching me, and that I wasn't welcomed there. But again, I felt like I had kind of a duty to record this stuff, so I kept going.

"There's a big rock pile you have to climb over and then you're inside this cavern, and inside the cavern is the shaft. Right away I knew this energy was coming from the shaft. I felt a freezing cold wind coming from it and I actually heard whispers. At this point I was really disturbed so I left.

"I checked the recordings when I got back and when I was walking down the first tunnel you could hear a few words in another language that sounded like Chinese. That would absolutely make sense because it was Asian miners who had worked there. I had a friend of mine from China listen to it and he translated it as 'let him go.' And in the background, almost constantly, you could hear a tapping sound, like a hammer. Again, for me it was totally silent, this was all picked up by the EVP recorder.

"The tapping got louder and louder as I got closer to the shaft, and then when I'm standing by the shaft you can hear a whole bunch of mumbling, in what sounds like maybe Cantonese, but my friend couldn't pick anything else out. There was a scream, too, that kind of sounded like a rusty metal door opening. And then there was a voice in English that was hard to make out, but it sounds like 'come down here.' I'm glad I didn't stay in there much longer, because like I said, there was some very strong, very dark energy in there, and I got the impression that there was something, human or not, trying to lure me in."

As a side note, Perdomo also delved into some of

his personal theories as to why Orcas Island seems to experience such a high degree of paranormal activity:

"I've done a lot of reading over the years, about mysticism, religion, I mean I've read the Bible, grimoires, the *Ars Goetia*, *Liber 777*, you name it, all just to try and explain the things that are unexplainable. I think Orcas is just at an intersection of a lot of different factors. It's crossed by ley lines, what the Native Americans call 'spirit paths,' there's a vortex right off Indian Island if you believe in that stuff, and there's a spring on the beach there, too, with healing properties. And if you look at island history, you see that limestone was one of the main industries in the old days. Limestone is considered a conductor for psychic energy, which goes into psychometry and the Stone Tape theory. Orcas is built on limestone.

"I've heard a theory, locally, that's pretty far out there, but it's basically that all this mining that went on may have released all this psychic energy that was stored in the rock, like poking holes in a […] dam. [Orcas] is supposed to have been part of Atlantis, as crazy as that sounds, and they're saying that all the spiritual or psychic energy or whatever you want to call it is still here. A lot of people think there's a lot of quartz under the island, too, and especially in Mount Constitution, people say there's a huge crystal that acts like a beacon. I don't know about that, but when you consider all these factors, you're left with one conclusion, that no matter how you look at it, Orcas is a highly spiritual place."

As Perdomo states, there is no shortage of mysterious mineralogy on Orcas Island. Some have pointed to the island's widespread deposits of quartz, tourmaline, titanite, silica, zircon, and other crystals as a possible explanation for the longtime reports of "ghost lights" and related phenomena. New Age theories notwithstanding, these crystals are known to conduct piezoelectricity, a type of current channeled up through the soil in the form of "earth lights," which have long been interpreted as supernatural in origin. Some have pointed to piezoelectricity as a possible explanation for the phenomena long observed at Ghost Rock, where a mysterious light has been seen dancing around the summit of the dry and rocky hill; a place where swamp gas is not a plausible factor (see the "Ghost Rock and Other Tales" chapter of this book).

Similarly, the Tectonic Strain Theory, developed by Dr. Michael Persinger and Dr. John S. Derr, holds that all manner of paranormal phenomena—ranging from UFOs to ghosts and the aforementioned "spook lights"—are in fact caused by electro-magnetic fields, themselves a product of tectonic activity. According to Persinger and Derr, these disturbances could potentially cause hallucinations and other unstable conditions of the brain. Considering that Orcas Island sits above numerous fault lines, and has a long history of small earthquakes, many interested islanders find the theory credible.

It's something in the water is a phrase often used in jest, but on Orcas it may have a truer meaning. Traces of petroleum were found in a Crow Valley well in 1947, and a Tacoma outfit drilled for oil there in 1958. A sulphur spring once flowed near Cascade Lake in the early days of white settlement—the healing properties of which were considered remarkable enough for its one-time owner, Dr. I.M. Harrison of Madrona Point, to draw up plans for a sanitarium. Cold Spring, high on the rim of Mount Constitution, once gushed from a rock that was set like an altar amid a particularly idyllic marsh. Though the spring ran dry many years ago, it is speculated to have been artesian; flowing from the distant Cascade Mountains through deep channels beneath the seabed.

The small spring on the beach below the Outlook Inn, too, was long known for its remarkable purity and mineral content. The spring, which once provided water for the Inn, was enclosed in a cement cistern in the early 1900s—and among the New Age inhabitants of the Outlook, inspired rumors of "healing prop-erties," as Perdomo put it. According to these spiritual types, the spring, which welled up from the furthest crystalline caverns of inner earth, was akin to the "vortex" so often spoken of by the Outlook coterie. Today, drinking from the ancient and crumbling cistern is hardly advisable, if the algae-green discharge that trickles down to the sea is any indication of its current cleanliness.

How does the odd geology of Orcas Island influence the strange phenomena so often reported here? Do the quartz-crystals in the Mount Constitution mines vibrate with some strange and psychic energy? Is there something deep in the rock that calls down the lightning, as James F. Tulloch suggested in his diary? And what bizarre curative qualities, if any, might be found in the waters that stream from the stony bowels of the island? These questions, and others, might only be answered by a visit to the little rivulets that burble down from the mountainside—a visit to the mines, where one might meet a fate similar to the fabled Chinese miners, is not recommended.

The Spooks of Nordstrom's Lane

Nordstrom's Lane is a narrow farm road that stretches across the windswept fields of Crow Valley,
connecting two of the island's main highways and
providing access to a handful of old farmsteads. As
short as it is—just over half a mile—Nordstrom's
Lane has a long and supposedly bloody history that
has given it a rather spooky reputation over the past
century, and as the following stories illustrate, this
unassuming thoroughfare lays claim to some of more
chilling paranormal activity recorded on Orcas Island.

The lane's disturbing history begins with a grisly
farm accident. A young farmhand is said to have been
crushed by a steam traction engine in the early 1900s,
while another version alleges that he was pulled into a
threshing machine and spewed out with the chaff.
This tragedy would have taken place within sight of

the lane.

Nordstrom's Lane would be the site of several vehicular accidents over the years, particularly at the intersection with the Horseshoe Highway; a point long known as "Dead Man's Corner" for the many motorists who have overshot the curve and careened into oblivion.

These incidents have resulted in a myriad of ghostly tales, such as the phantom headlights said to follow travelers down the road at odd hours of the night, and the mangled apparition seen wandering in the mist that often blankets the valley. Supposedly, the specter of a man—presumably the maimed farmhand—will appear on misty nights, standing by the side of the road, his limbs bent at unnatural angles and his head crushed flat, before he vanishes back into the dark. One lifelong islander, Sandra Yates*, detailed her family's odd encounter, which took place in 2016:

We were coming back from the ferry one night and we had just turned down Nordstrom when all of a sudden the atmosphere felt very different. There was fog in the valley and behind us I could see a pair of headlights. The headlights followed closely behind us all the way to the turnoff onto Crow Valley road, where we turned right. I looked in the mirror to see which way the headlights would turn, but they were totally gone. I had only looked away for a split second.

Amateur ghost-hunter and Orcas resident Shane

Anderson also had a strange story to tell:

"Yeah, I grew up hearing about Nordstrom's Lane and all the weird stuff that supposedly happens down there, so me and some buddies went out there back in our senior year, so I guess 2010, because we wanted to see if it was true [...] so we went out there at three a.m., you know, the devil's hour, and we just cruised down the road real slow to see what would happen. And right away, we noticed that our electronics started acting all janky. My boy Tristin tried to call his girl just to, like, mess with her, but he didn't have any service, and then we all checked and none of us did. Which is weird because normally it's pretty good out there. And then, this is crazy, one of my subwoofers blew out. Like, brand new sub-woofers. So I'm like [...] let's get out of here.

"So I hit a U-turn at the stop sign by Crow Valley and I basically floored it, just trying to get back to the highway without any more weird stuff happening. Like halfway down the road, by this old barn, these headlights just appeared behind us, like I don't know where they could have come from, and they started mad-dogging us down the road. I was looking in the mirror the whole time and I couldn't see a truck behind them, just the two lights. We all start yelling like, 'this dude's going to try to run us off the road,' but they disappeared as soon as we got to the highway [...] it can be a pretty easy shortcut, but I've never been back there."

Anderson was kind enough to connect the author with local musician and woodworker Iver Kinney, who had an unusual experience of his own on Nordstrom's Lane:

Me and my girlfriend Chloe went there at night just on a chill night drive. After jamming with some friends in Deer Harbor and hitting the bubbler a little bit, haha. But when we turned down Nordstrom's Lane everything changed. There was mist in the valley and we saw a guy standing on the side of the road. We only saw him for a sec because of the mist but me and Chloe both agreed on what we saw.

It was his head. It looked like it was run over with a tank or something. It was bloody and flat like a pancake and you could barely recognize that he even had a face at all. After that, I don't want to say I drove recklessly, but I'm gonna say we booked it going as fast as possible through that mist. I've never felt like that before and I don't want to again, and honestly I see that thing in my nightmares.

The idea of a haunted road is, in some ways, even more frightening than that of a haunted house; Nordstrom's Lane is a sunny and iconic place, well-known to photographers and sightseers for its old-world aesthetic. But later, when the fog begins to pool in the valley bottom and drift across the road, the tall grass and the scattered groves darken, and a traveler begins to wonder what horrors might be lurking there, waiting to shamble forth . . .

UFOs and Other Phenomena

Have spacemen from beyond the moon ever visited Orcas? Since 1947, islanders have reported weird lights and other strange things in the sky, leading some to label Orcas a "UFO hotspot" or even a "window area"—a place where otherworldly beings slip across our dimensional plane. This should come as little surprise, given that Washington itself was ranked first in UFO sightings by the National UFO Reporting Center, and that Orcas, despite its relatively small landmass, is allegedly home to so many other bizarre things.

The first whispers of weird craft on Orcas arose at the tail-end of the "flying disc craze" of 1947. In July of that year, five "sober and reliable" citizens sighted a massive, otherworldly craft in the skies over North

Beach. As the *Orcas Islander* reported:

At an hour shortly before 10 o'clock Tuesday evening, July 22, Howard Wilson, his son-in-law, Blaine Rogers of Spokane, Reuben Wallstrom of Richmond, Cal., and Wesley Langell were at the Wilson cottage on North Beach when Mr. Wilson saw something in the sky in the general direction of the Saturna light, but much higher up, which lit up the sky. At the same instant Wesley Langell saw it also. Mr. Wilson says it looked to him like the hub cap of a gigantic automobile wheel. It was clearly visible for about three seconds and then disappeared in a bright flash.

Mr. Langell says it looked "sort of spooky." Messrs. Wallstrom and Rogers say that they saw only the light, which was brilliant and could not possibly be confused with the Saturna light. All four agree that as it faded out the light was moving rapidly to the north.

At the time the party knew that Thad McGlinn was fishing off the north shore, but none of them saw or communicated with him until the next morning, when Howard Wilson went into Templin's store and said: "Thad, did you see anything unusual on the north shore last night?"

"Why, no," McGlinn replied, "except that funny bright light off to the north. It sure was unusual."

So that makes five that saw the flying disc.

The craze continued into 1948, as Kenneth Arnold visited the old Olympic Lodge in Deer Harbor. Arnold, an aviator, had made headlines the year before with his report of flying saucers over Mount

Rainier—widely considered the first such sighting in history, as well as the seeming catalyst for the strange summer of 1947, which had culminated with the famed Roswell crash in New Mexico. Arnold's visit to Orcas was comparatively uneventful, with no flying discs reported.

The island's first recorded UFO sighting—aside from the craft commonly observed at the Outlook Inn—was in August of 1974, when Joe Dalton*, Anthony Heimbach*, and Doug Morris* encountered an unearthly lightshow on Point Lawrence Road. Dalton, who often recounted the story at the old Teezer's Coffee Shop, wrote the following in correspondence with the author:

It was late in the summer of '74 and I would have been a junior in high school then. Me, Doug, and Anthony were coming back from a day of messing around at Steve Larson's dirt track in my old pickup, with Douggy's Bultaco in the back . . . he'd been doing burnouts like a jackass and ended up wiping out and ripped the pipe out of his cylinder and cracked it at the same time. So all three of us crammed in the truck and we headed out at around 8:30, right after sunset.

We were almost to the straightaway at Bond's mill when all of a sudden the cab filled with a bright red light. I was so surprised that I hit the brakes and stopped dead in the road. I suppose my first thought was that it was the sheriff pulling us over because, I'm ashamed to say it, we'd all had more than a few beers that night. But no, that wasn't it . . . it was off in the woods towards Mt. Pickett, and it wasn't any cop's siren . . .

Ol' Heimbach decided he wanted to get a better look and he got out, much to my chagrin, because I didn't know what the hell it was. When he touched the door handle he got an electric shock. The air was crackling with static electricity and I could feel my hair standing on end, like touching one of those plasma balls.

We watched that light for a minute or two, until the shadows started changing and we realized it was starting to move. The light floated up above the trees and we could see it now, a bright ball of red light, and it hung there in the air for a few seconds before it changed color into white . . . and then it shot off into the sky going east at about a million miles an hour. It was gone in the blink of an eye, and just like that all the electricity in the air was gone and my hair flopped back down again. We all looked at each other and said, "Let's get the hell out of here," and that's just what we did.

To this day none of us knows exactly what it is we saw that night, but I can tell you it's nothing you'll find in a science book. That much I am sure of.

Indeed, such activity seems to be centered around the eastern lobe of Orcas, particularly the area around Moran State Park. Mount Constitution, after all, is said to contain a massive crystal which attracts paranormal phenomena, at least according to the New Agers who settled here in the 1960s (see the "Mysterious Mount Constitution" chapter of this book). Locals have long reported lights in the sky that move at impossible angles and with incredible speed, making ninety-degree turns and other maneuvers of which no aircraft is capable, and of huge objects gliding over the remote ridges surrounding Mount Constitution with no audible sound.

Four years after Dalton's encounter, an entire room full of diners at the Rosario Mansion witnessed a bizarre light show over Cascade Bay. In February of 1978, Deputy Roger Dixon received a report of a "bright, very intense light over the water" that was seen by several staff members and patrons alike. According to a waiter named Charles Grass, the "object" appeared at around seven o'clock and was plainly visible from the dining room's massive windows.

Grass said that it was directly left of the Orion constellation's three-starred belt by about three "belt lengths." It was no larger than the north star, he said, though others said it was larger.

Employees and guests began flocking to the windows to observe the phenomenon. Julie Brackett, a reservations desk clerk, gave a more detailed account:

"I went into the Vista Lounge and used the binoculars. What I saw was larger and closer than what Charles described. The colors were red, blue, green, and yellow, like several hundred small, different-colored lights, sparkling rather than flashing. It was the size of a small airplane, but it definitely was not an airplane. I estimated it was about 2,500 feet. I didn't see it move, but I only watched it for three minutes.

"The shape was indefinite. There was a slight haze in the sky that night, and it appeared around 7:00 or

8:00 p.m. I know it was a week night, three to five weeks ago.

"We reported it to the UFO center in Seattle, and were later informed by them that there were no planes or helicopters in the area at the time of the sighting.

"Later that night, when I went home, the sky was perfectly clear and I saw an object in the sky that had a definite shape. This bright object was very large and so much brighter than the stars. Its shape was clearly that of an inverted 'V' which shone brightly. A pointed mass was in the neck of the V was in a deep blue.

"I saw the same thing I saw at Rosario about eight months ago from my home on Orcas, and that bright V-shaped object was also visible in the sky that night. I haven't seen either thing in the sky since the night of the Rosario sighting."

Brackett speculated that the object might have been a satellite that was somehow "enlarged" through an optical illusion.

"I'm not saying that I believe absolutely that there is something unusual behind these things," she said, "but after seeing them, it makes you a little more of a believer."

Notably, a couple living on Shaw Island's Broken Point had reported identical phenomena on the same evening—they had even filed a report with the Sheriff's Office. This seeming spate of sightings prompted the *Journal* to launch an investigation of their own; and an anonymous phone call received a few days after their initial article seemed poised to break the case.

The tipster told reporter Deborah M. Smith that a Rosario resident named Gary Bauder may have been responsible for the "hoax." Bauder was an electronics expert who had previously coordinated laser shows and holographic displays for local venues.

"It was easier for the anonymous tipster to believe that this young man had created an illusion in the sky than any other explanation for the strange sightings," wrote Smith.

Bauder denied the accusations. While he *did* own a laser, he said, and had the capability to project holograms on a small scale, nothing he possessed was powerful enough to create the display seen at Rosario —and certainly nothing that could be seen six miles away on Shaw.

Bauder, in fact, had a UFO story of his own. The year before, he and four friends had been relaxing at his parents' home overlooking Rosario. Bauder had been demonstrating his laser, he said, and had decided to call it a night, when all of a sudden the darkened room was "bathed in a bright light for three seconds." The five friends leaped for the windows and tore open the curtains.

The friends saw a massive object in the sky, "between Mount Constitution and Rosario Palisades Hill, almost directly over the lake," said Bauder. It was "oval, with a bright, glowing white-red center," and was as large as "half a city block." The glow "phased into hues, colors like I'd never seen before," he continued. The object hung in the sky for a few seconds before beginning to slowly descend—and then it "split really fast, leaving what looked like a comet tail for 15 seconds. But it was going in the opposite direction that a comet would go," Bauder added.

He saw it once more, at around nine-thirty on another night, as he descended Palisades Road below the Cascade Lake lagoon. The object was farther away this time, and was "simply passing through."

Bauder reflected: "For that moment, I was confronted with something that to my knowledge could not have been fabricated on earth. I had to accept the possibility that it was extraterrestrial."

Around twenty years later, Theresa Nyland had a series of mystifying encounters while living near Doe Bay. One night, while returning to her home on the southern slopes of Mount Pickett, she observed a flash of light somewhere beyond the summit that was bright enough to illuminate the trees along the ridgeline for hundreds of yards. Though curious as to what the source could have been, since it came from an isolated part of the state park, she thought little of it until a few nights later, when she saw the flash again, this time in the company of a neighbor.

"It was bright enough that it felt like looking at the sun," says Theresa.

"[My neighbor] and I both happened to be standing in the driveway when we saw the flash [...] like before, it was just behind the top of the ridge, where there are no houses or campgrounds, or even trails that I know of. There was no sound of any kind, in fact the frogs and the night birds had gone totally quiet, but I don't know how to describe it . . . the light pulsed through us, like a shockwave almost. But the ground didn't shake. Our bodies vibrated, is the only way I can think to put it."

Theresa's most vivid encounter would come a month or two later, however. While sitting on her porch overlooking the moonlit Rosario Strait, Theresa began to feel an "electricity" in the air, in a detail that is remarkably similar to Joe Dalton's tale—which Theresa denies having heard prior. Glancing up, she was astonished to see a massive black object blotting out the stars overhead!

"It was triangular, and I couldn't guess how big it was because I had no frame of reference," she said. "It almost looked like a void. There were no lights or any kind of reflection. It was moving slow, like when you see an airliner, but I think it was at a fairly low altitude. It took about ten minutes to pass over my house and go over the ridge, and then I couldn't see it anymore."

Afterwards, Theresa claims to have observed an increase in the usual military traffic, including low-flying Prowler jets and Black Hawk helicopters in

Homeland Security livery.

"They buzzed my house more than once," says Theresa. "It seemed like they were looking for something."

In the state park itself, visitors have reported similar phenomena for decades, including a mysterious hum that permeates the air with no apparent source.

"We had a lot of people ask about the hum," says former Moran camp host Keith Guindon,

". . . but we never have a good answer for them [...] you'll hear it in different places, I heard it once near the burn piles [*Author's Note: located off the service road near Hidden Falls*]. It's just a hum like you would hear standing next to a power station. I couldn't tell where it was coming from, though . . . it's like it was all around me, like the air itself was humming, if that makes sense [...] you could really feel it [...] I've had people tell me they heard it in a lot of different places, one couple said they heard it on top of the mountain, one guy said it was by [Mountain Lake] . . . I've heard a lot of crazy theories on what it could be."

Other tales from the park include "fireballs" darting through the night sky and unknown craft akin to Theresa Nyland's account. One longtime islander mentioned having seen a trio of small, silvery craft pass over Mountain Lake, something supposedly witnessed by a number of other people at the campground.

The most peculiar accounts, however, originate with the mysterious Polarity Institute at Doe Bay. The Polarity people allegedly claimed to have established telepathic communications with off-world beings who had erected a secret base within the park. These beings, benevolent in nature, sought only to observe humanity for scientific purposes, and to impart their cosmic wisdom onto a select few humans—the Institute's researchers, of course, being among them. A former follower, known by her spiritual name of "Rupasatra," operated informal "UFO tours" of the park even years after the Institute's disbandment.

Perry Bishop, an Anacortes resident and avid sailor, was taking friends on a cruise through the islands aboard his 31-foot ketch when they spotted an unusual aerial display. The party, under sail near Matia Island, observed at least three "orbs" in the clouds over Mount Constitution.

"We watched these [...] orbs, I would call them [...] for about seven or eight minutes," says Bishop. "They were orangeish-white and I would say they must have been glowing in some way, for them to be visible against the clouds . . . they floated around the mountaintop slowly, almost like moths on a lightbulb, just kind of aimlessly. Eventually we lost track of them."

The UFOs allegedly return, now and again, to the site of their first visitation. In 2017, tourists relaxing at North Beach claimed to have sighted three fireballs floating overhead in a triangular formation, before the phenomenon moved out to sea toward Sucia Island and flew straight up into the sky. A few miles away, at the old Glenwood Inn, lights were spotted at a very high altitude, making impossible turns and covering huge distances in a split-second. The lights disappeared as dawn approached.

A Flaherty's Hill-area resident, Ted Lister, recounted having seen a "satellite"-type object moving through the night sky, at a normal pace, before it zipped away at a ninety-degree angle, leaving Ted dumbfounded.

Just what is it that people have reported sighting here for the past fifty years? Are these "objects" extraterrestrial in origin, or are they something else entirely? And, perhaps most importantly, can these accounts be written off as hoaxes? Who can say . . . but the next time you're out stargazing on a clear night, and the stars begin to move, it couldn't hurt to ask, is that *really* a satellite whizzing past up there?

Pennies from Heaven

The old Donohue place on North Beach Road, about a half mile outside Eastsound, has stood for over one hundred and thirty years, and will likely stand for as many more—a testament to the skills of its builder, the master carpenter Michael S. Donohue. The old farmhouse has weathered many changes over the years, including a brief stint as a hostel, but has remained relatively true to its original form. And as we shall see, its long legacy has invited a rich history of hauntings, as well.

The Donohues first came to Orcas in 1883 and homesteaded at the present-day site of the Sportsmen Club. In 1890, he purchased a one-hundred-and-eighty-acre tract from Walter E. Sutherland on North Beach Road and built the two-story farmhouse, in addition to planting an extensive apple orchard that still exists, in part, today. Donohue found considerable success on Orcas, as both a carpenter and a civic leader; he built the Episcopal and Methodist churches in Eastsound, with his friend Peter Bostian, and later served as county commissioner and Master of the Grange. A Civil War veteran of the 120th New York Infantry, he attended the 50th anniversary celebrations at the Gettysburg battlefield, which reunited G.A.R. and Confederate veterans for a six-day jubilee.

Michael Donohue would eventually give the house to his son Harry, and his new wife Jean, and it was to remain in the family for many decades. A notable chapter of this period was the residency of Lieutenant Colonel John Black Vliet, who stayed with the Donohues for several years at the turn of the century. Vliet, born in 1822, had enjoyed a long and distinguished career as a surveyor and civil engineer in his native Wisconsin, before commissioning as a Captain in the 31st Wisconsin Infantry in 1862. Vliet had quite the colorful service during the war, being captured by rebel forces near Acworth, Georgia in June of 1864 and subsequently escaping back to Union lines. In 1865 he was commissioned as a Lieutenant Colonel of the 51st Wisconsin Infantry, and served in that capacity until the end of the war.

Colonel Vliet retired to the San Juans in the mid-1890s and stayed with a fellow Wisconsin officer named Elvin Haworth Smith, the "Hermit of Matia," who had built a cabin on Matia Island and lived there as its sole inhabitant. Smith was a well-known figure in the area and was hardly a recluse despite living alone—he had developed a reputation as a healer who could cure a wide variety of illnesses through "Therapeutic Suggestion" and telepathy. He would return from his weekly trips to Orcas's north shore with buckets of letters from afflicted persons nationwide, who swore that Smith was able to cure them through the mail using only the power of the mind and "God's law," as Smith put it. Vliet lived with Smith for an unknown time and then moved to Orcas, allegedly after a quarrel over who'd been the superior general during the war—Grant or Sherman. Smith and another Civil War veteran, George Carrier, would vanish while crossing between Orcas and Matia in 1921.

John B. Vliet lived with Harry and Jean Donohue for several years before moving back to Wisconsin in 1909, where he would pass away the following year. Some believe that it is Vliet's spirit that inhabits the old Donohue place.

"I was told there's a friendly ghost in the house," says Aspen Craighead, who stayed at the house while it was a hostel in 2014,

". . . and I kind of said, 'yeah, sure.' But my first night there, in the co-ed dorm, I heard someone walking down the hall outside the room. I thought it was my friend Kai, since we were basically the only ones there, so I went out to look and [...] there was no one there. Kai was still asleep.

"I asked one of the staff about it the next morning and they started laughing and said, 'yeah, that's just the Colonel, making his rounds.'

"[...] After that, not much else happened, because we were only there for a few days, but I smelled pipe tobacco a few times, out of nowhere, and I guarantee no one else was smoking around there."

Aspen's account is echoed by a former staff member of the now-defunct hostel, Jordan Foster*, who related a few odd encounters of his own.

"We used to smell pipesmoke all the time, yeah. It smelled nice. Kind of reminded me of my grandpa," says Jordan. "The weirdest thing was that we would always find pennies scattered around in different places. I don't even know where they came from. Most of them were wheat pennies, so I was always looking to see if they had valuable mint marks."

Jordan chuckles. "Someone told me that pennies are easy for ghosts to move around because of the copper. I guess copper, as an element, is easier for ghosts to move, as opposed to the other elements [...] it's just too bad they can't move dollar coins . . ."

Colonel Vliet's may not be the only specter at the Donohue place. The ghostly presence of a woman was often reported, and hostel staff began calling the spirit "Myra," after Michael Donohue's wife.

"I stayed there for a week, and I can say with absolute certainty that there is a female presence in that house," writes Taylor Phelps, another former guest. "It doesn't feel scary so much as it does watchful. I believe the spirit is a proud woman who is still watching over her beloved home, making sure the modern guests don't make too much of a mess."

Taylor further recounts finding her shoes moved and carefully rearranged under her bed, and witnessing the back door swing open and then carefully shut again, all of its own accord.

"The room filled with the scent of rose perfume," writes Taylor, ". . . and then, as soon as the door had closed, the scent faded away."

Do the spirits of Myra and Colonel Vliet still inhabit the old Donohue place? As of this writing, the hostel has closed and the home is now a private residence—meaning the privacy of the new owners should be respected at all costs—and so, for the average amateur investigator, the answer will most likely never be known. Still, one wonders if the Union Colonel and the Rebel Major at the Outlook Inn ever meet in their ghostly wanderings and scrap it out for old time's sake . . .

Blood on the Stone Club

In the haze of the very distant past, Orcas Island was the site of wars, romances, and intrigue to equal anything found in the great tomes of Western literature. The famed photographer and ethnologist Edward Curtis made a study of one such legend in his 1913 work The North American Indian, Volume 9, *which is reprinted here in full:*

Hutahlim, who lived in a Lummi village on Orcas Island, one day quarreled with his Skolahun wife, and drove her away.

"Go home," he said, "and live with your brothers, and let them feed you steelhead trout for your fat legs!"

When the woman got home, she told her brothers how she had been driven away and twitted about her fat legs, and insultingly accused of living on steelhead trout. In time Hutahlim recovered from his anger and decided to go and become reconciled with his wife. He asked his youthful brother Shalaktst to accompany him. They launched a canoe and proceeded to Lummi Bay, where the older man told his brother to remain in the canoe with the slave and to keep it afloat as the tide ebbed, so that if the people made trouble Hutahlim could effect a quick retreat.

When the people saw Hutahlim approaching, one said, "There is someone coming." The woman replied, "That is my husband." Her brothers quickly told her to treat him well, and when there was a good opportunity they would kill him because of what he had said about them in the matter of the steelhead trout. She took up the mat she was weaving, carried it halfway to the water, and sat down to work. Her husband sat beside her, and they talked as if nothing had happened to disturb their relations. After a while she made him lay his head in her lap, and she loused him. But all the while she was twisting his hair tightly in her hands.

"Are you finding many?" he asked.

"No," said the woman.

"What are you doing with my hair?"

"I am just looking for them."

Then she uttered a cry, and her brothers came running. Hutahlim leaped up, but the woman clung to his hair. He ran toward the canoe, dragging her behind, but they quickly overtook and killed him.

Meanwhile the youth had been watching, and he kept working his canoe out into the water. He saw how his brother fell, and how his head was cut off. Then he paddled homeward. At the most easterly point of Orcas Island, he said to the slave:

"Go home and tell my mother what has happened. I am going into the mountains to see what I can do. There I will stay until I find something. If I do not return, you will know that I am dead."

The slave carried the news to the village, and the people began to mourn; but they decided to take no action until they saw what the youth would do.

For three days, Shalaktst washed himself in the salt water, rubbing first with sharp leaves to make the blood run, and then with leaves containing juice that made the wounds burn. Next he made a raft, and a cedar-bark rope to which he tied a large stone as if for an anchor. He pushed out into the water off the point, and taking the stone in his hands he dived from the raft. There on the bottom of the sea a person spoke to him, saying: "I have not what you want. But if you will go on the hill, there will be a person who will give it to you."

When the youth came to himself he was lying high and dry on the beach. He walked up to a lake on the mountaintop, and there he made another raft and another anchor-line, and in the middle of the lake he plunged downward with the stone. He heard these words: "I have not what you want; but if you will go to the next place below, there is a small pool where you will find it."

Recovering consciousness, the youth remembered what he had been told, and went down toward East Sound. He looked for a lake, but found only a small marsh, and though he searched for a deep pool, there was none. The water was covered with pond-lillies, and he could not find a place to dive, so he threw himself flat on his face. In the water he saw an old man who said: "I understand that you have been having bad luck. You have a great enemy to face. Here is what you need. Take great care of it. Let no one handle it. You will not have to pursue your enemies; they will come up to you and you will club them with this. To prove that this weapon is good, you may remove the cover and wave the club in the air, and the place will be filled with a fog, so that you cannot see."

When Shalaktst awoke, he was on the edge of the swamp with a weapon in his hand—a stone club as long as a man's forearm. He made a covering of cedar-bark and started homeward, and in the woods behind the village he hid the weapon in a crotch of a standing cedar. The people were happy to see him return, but none asked any questions as to what plans he had. Everybody, however, made preparations, mending their canoes and their weapons.

"Why are you doing this?" asked Shalaktst. And they replied: "We are prepared for whatever you say. If you are ready to take vengeance, we will go with you and make war."

"We will start tomorrow in the morning," he

announced.

Early in the morning they embarked in ten large war-canoes. Just before they pushed off, the young man said: "I do not wish to deceive you and take you far away to lose your lives, but to prove that I have something with which to fight I will show you what I have." He took out the club, removed the cover, and waved the weapon over his head. In an instant the bay was obscured with fog. This exhibition put the people in good spirits, and they started.

They landed at Lummi Bay, and were informed by some stragglers on the beach that the Skolahun had gone away, fearing vengeance. So they went around the point into Bellingham Bay. At the port-age across the peninsula they heard a sound as of a paddle beating on the water, and they knew what it was. A Lummi man who had married a Skolahun woman was in the habit of setting his nets for flounders and then beating on the water with a pole on the end of which was a wooden slab, thus frightening the flounders in toward the nets. The warriors moved toward the sound, and when they found the fisherman they asked where the people were. He said, "They are all at Hwuhlkeyum" [*Author's note: a village at the mouth of the Nooksack River at present-day Marietta -Alderwood*]. They told him to come into one of the canoes, and his companion, a Skolahun, they ordered to remain where he was.

They proceeded to Fish Point, and Shalaktst said to his people: "Let all the canoes remain here, and I will go alone to see what is there. When I give the war-cry, then you may come up, but not before." He went into the village and entered a house, passing a large dog, and concealed himself behind a bundle of mat material. Near the door a woman was cooking flounders. The house sheltered several families. The dog got up, and lay down beside the woman, who turned and struck him with the fire-stick, saying, "Go out, you long-faced Shalaktst!"

When Shalaktst heard this insult, he went to the woman and picked up the stick on which the roasting flounders were spitted. "Let me see your face," he said. And as she turned, he slapped her on the face with the hot flounders. Then the people aroused themselves, and Shalaktst said: "I am Shalaktst, and if you want to measure my face to see how long it is, now is the time to do it!"

He took out his war-club, and as they sat there motionless at the sight of it he went about the house and killed them one by one, the slightest touch of the stone weapon sufficing.

Now the fisherman had told him that behind the houses there was a plank bridge along which the people would rush to escape into the woods. At this place he stationed himself and uttered the war-cry. His warriors on the beach answered, and the villagers made a rush for the bridge. But at the upper end stood Shalaktst, and he clubbed them down one after the other. The bodies piled up on both sides of the bridge until he could not reach those who were still coming in flight from the war-party, and he leaped over the heap to meet them. Thus he made success-sively three great piles of corpses. By this time the Lummi had reached the scene, but there was nothing left to do: for, except a very few who had escaped in another direction, all had been killed with the stone club. They stowed all the plunder in their own canoes as well as in those of the slain, and returned to Orcas Island, where they shared the booty with those who had remained at home.

Some time after this, Shalaktst heard that some of the Skolahun who had been living in a settlement where Marietta now stands had moved to the Lummi Bay village that he had found deserted. He was determined to exterminate them. There were only a few, and he went with a small party and killed all. Then he learned that a few families still lived on the Nooksack River. These had made it a rule to fish only at night, and each man would take in his canoe his daughter and his valuables, and at intervals he would cry out: "Shalaktst, I mean no harm! I am not of those people you have been killing. Here is my daughter and here are my treasures, which you may have."

One night Shalaktst came, intending to kill these families. Hearing the fishermen as they floated down the river with their nets, he ordered his men to run their canoes under the bank among the brush. After the Skolahun had passed, the Lummi paddled out and observed them lifting their nets. Shalaktst stood up and cried: "I am Shalaktst!" The people were astonished and frightened, and they begged so abjectly for mercy that he agreed to let them live.

The Lummi accompanied the fishermen to their homes, where presents were heaped up and given to the chief, along with the wife he had been promised. "I will take the woman and the gifts," he said, "but this will not be the final settlement. I must consult my people about the peace." They remained there that night, one man watching while the others slept. On the following day they returned to Orcas Island with the news that the remnant of the Skolahun desired peace and offered to yield their right to the river.

So on a day [sic] the Lummi moved toward the mainland. They camped first on the northern end of Lummi Island in houses belonging to the Samish, and this village they subsequently held, forcing the Samish to find other fishing grounds. After a while they crossed to the mainland and took possession, permitting the few remaining Skolahun to live and marry among them.

Curtis further writes:

Even as late as about 1830 the Lummi claimed, in addition to the mainland from Chuckanut Bay to Birch Bay, the following islands: Orcas, Blakely, Lopez (on the north and the west coast), Shaw, San Juan (except the west coast, and even that they held in earlier days), Spieden, Stuart, Waldron, and all the many islets in the waters thus defined.

Tales of the Orcas Island School District

Situated on a hill overlooking Eastsound, the Orcas Island School District has served Kindergarten through twelfth-grade students for well over one hundred years; a marked change from the early days, when students would congregate at log cabins or rough-hewn schoolhouses for their rudimentary lessons in reading and arithmetic. Most do not realize, however, that this modern façade is just that—a veneer, disguising a plethora of old secrets.

The school grounds are a stone's throw from the old Mount Baker Cemetery, one of the island's first burying grounds. Opened in 1890 as a replacement for the previous boneyard on Madrona Point, the first burials had been reinterments of the older graves—

namely a few Hudson's Bay trappers and their half-Indian progeny—and most were unidentified, as the wooden markers had long since rotted away. Many suspect that these remains were buried in a "potter's field" away from the main cemetery, and that some may have been covered over with the development of Buck Park and the school campus. In fact, that is exactly the case, according to a longtime islander and "witcher" named Tom Uhler.

Uhler had learned the skill of witching from his grandfather, who had migrated west from Kentucky and found success as a well-digger in Eastern Washington. Farmers and stockmen would hire the man to locate wells with the aid of his two L-shaped "witching rods," which, with one in each hand, would slowly cross in tandem when groundwater was underfoot.

"He made his money finding water, but he always said water wasn't the only thing you could witch for," says Uhler. "You could find minerals and graves, too."

During the Vietnam War, Uhler put his unusual skillset to use while serving in the Marines, using two rods fashioned from coat-hangers to locate a Viet Cong weapons cache and a number of "spider holes," for which he was awarded the Navy Achievement Medal with Combat "V" device.

"They didn't say *how* I found the tunnels, just that I found them," laughs Uhler.

Now, some fifty years later, Uhler claims to have located at least three sets of remains buried beneath the sports field on the Orcas Island campus.

"An old guy I used to have coffee with told me about the graves that were left behind […] when they moved the old cemetery," he says.

"Apparently there were some Hudson's Bay trappers who were buried there, and a couple of Indians, but that was thirty or forty years before they opened the Mount Baker Cemetery so the wood markers were long gone. They moved everyone with markers that they knew about but it was common knowledge that some got left.

"Now I mostly find wells, it's something I do for friends more as a hobby, but I decided I wanted to see if I could find these graves like my granddad used to do. He'd find Indians buried when he was looking for wells […] so I went out there one morning and just started walking around the football field. And pretty soon I felt the rods start to cross. They did that for six feet, and I thought, 'well, that's a grave.' I found two more of them after that.

"I went to the schoolboard and I told them, 'hey, I think I found some graves under your football field,' but I don't think they put a lot of stock in witching […] that, and they probably don't want to have to dig up their field."

Tall tale or not, the forgotten graves beneath the sports field appear to have influenced a number of spine-tingling accounts. Zak Perdomo, a "ghost hunter" who also investigated the Augusta Mine on Mount Constitution, visited the Orcas Island campus in 2018 and shared his experiences with the author:

"I wasn't able to get inside the actual buildings, but I did walk around the campus itself and record for EVPs [*Author's Note: "electronic voice phenomenon"*] where the bodies are supposed to be buried [...] I was out on the soccer field and right away I felt something was totally off. Very weird, very dark vibes. There was one spot where I stopped dead in my tracks because I felt the temperature drop like twenty degrees in a split second. It was like maybe a hundred yards from the grandstand, and I felt super uneasy. Keep in mind it was already a pretty cold and windy day, this was in, I think, late October, early November. So I stood there for a while, honestly fighting the urge to get out of there, and I took some photos and recorded. I found more cold spots after that. The temperature would go back to normal as soon as I walked a few feet away.

"I also felt a very uneasy presence coming from the forest behind the grandstand [...] it definitely felt like someone or something was watching me, in a very evil, kind of almost predatory way. There used to be a house on that land that I guess some pretty bad stuff happened in, so who knows. That's where April's Grove is now.

"On the way back to my car, I walked past the brick building, the elementary school, and I saw a shadow flit from one window to another on the second story. I took more photos and then I got out of there. I felt totally unwelcome.

"[The photos] show some really compelling stuff. There were a lot of orbs where I'd felt the cold spots, and in one of the photos I took of the elementary, you can see this really vivid streak that almost looks like a claw mark. Which to me almost suggests there's some kind of demonic activity, but who knows.

"I got a couple of EVPs, as well. It's actually pretty difficult to make out because of how windy it was when I was recording, but you can hear at least two voices. Both of them I don't think are speaking English [...] I've been told it might be a Native American language [...] from what I've researched about it, I guess there were a couple of French-Canadian, like mountain men who were buried there in the 1800s, and also some Native Americans. It's hard to find info beyond what people were told by their grandparents or whatever."

The sports field is hardly the only haunted spot on campus, however—the old place is just as spooky indoors as it is out. The first schoolhouse on the site was constructed at the turn of the century, standing two and a half stories tall, with grammar school classes on the first floor and high school on the second. It served its purpose until the Nellie S. Milton building was erected in 1949, followed by the Old Gym in 1957 and the separate Middle and High School facilities forty-four years later. They are fine, sturdy buildings, and each lay claim to purported phenomena of the spine-tingling variety.

Janine Sedgley*, a longtime substitute teacher, reported a few unnerving events during her time at the high school. In one instance, while reviewing a lesson plan after hours, Janine claimed to have heard several lockers on the second floor open and slam shut at once. In another, while sitting in the biology room with the door open, she heard the distinct sound of someone walking down the hallway outside, complete with the "swishing" of fabric on legs. Janine looked up as the footsteps approached the door, but she saw nothing as the footsteps passed and continued down the hall.

"I always get a weird feeling in there," says Janine.

Nellie S. Milton Elementary lays claim to its fair share of spooky goings-on, as well. A former principal, Greg Fitch*, had an unusual encounter that left him shaken for days afterward. In his own words:

"I was in my office working late, probably getting close to midnight, and I heard a big, big commotion coming from upstairs. Room above me was a classroom and there shouldn't have been anyone up there [...] I was alone in the school at that point [...] so I went upstairs. I had to unlock the door, and it was totally dark, no sounds at all. I cleared the whole room and I didn't find anything [...] it sounded like someone had been moving desks around but everything was normal [...] I called the sheriff and they did a sweep of the whole place but they didn't find anyone or any signs of a break-in [...] I'm still confused by that."

Greg also mentioned a few other odd occurrences, namely books falling off the shelves in the school library and the occasional sounds of a phantom basketball bouncing on the floor of the Old Gym when the place was deserted.

"I'd hear a basketball bounce as I'd be locking up," says Greg. "And when I'd look behind me, of course there wouldn't be anyone there. I'd hear squeaks like shoes scuffing on the floor sometimes. I'm sure that was just me hearing things if I didn't sleep well enough the night before."

Regardless of whether the stories are true or not, the Orcas Island School District is certainly home to more than a few spine-tingling tales. Is not the notion that your future resting place may be turned into a soccer field chilling enough?

Camp Spirit

Summer camps have long been fodder for ghostly legends, and the two on Orcas Island, Camp Orkila and Camp Four Winds, are certainly no exception. Both camps have extensive histories and are said to host a variety of spine-tingling tales.

Camp Orkila, the oldest sleepaway on the island, was established by the YMCA in 1906, on a property owned by the prominent Colman family of Seattle. The land, a sprawling old-growth forest overlooking Waldron Island and President Channel, was ideal for nurturing the ideals of self-reliance and woodcraft, and proved to be a great success. Only thirty boys attended the first season in 1906, but by the 1920s that number had swelled into the hundreds.

The land's history stretches back much farther

than these first turn-of-the-century excursions, however. The tract which would eventually become Camp Orkila was once situated between two Indian villages, *Xoxolos* near West Beach, and *Tlqwoloqs* at Point Doughty. Jim Kirkpatrick, a counselor for a number of seasons in the 1970s, elaborated on the camp's history in correspondence with the author:

I first came to Orkila in the early 60s, back before they let girls in, and back when you had to sell soap door-to-door just to raise the money. It was a lot different back then, as I'm sure you can imagine! I was a city kid growing up in Seattle and there was nothing better than piling on the buses at the North-gate Mall and taking the ferry out to Orcas. I liked it so much that I hired on as a counselor, and I was there every summer from 1971 through 1975.

[...] When I was a camper there, the counselors had a lot of stories they used to tell to try and scare the bejeezus out of us kids. Telling them now they might seem kind of hokey, but when the campfire is roaring and the woods are dark, they get a whole lot scarier, let me tell you . . .

One story that sticks in my mind is the legend of He-Who-Eats. We had a counselor named Jerry who had a real way with words, and he was the guy I really tried to pattern myself after when I became a counselor myself. A real straight arrow guy, but a lot of fun to be around, too. Jerry would tell this story about how before the land became Orkila, it was considered a dark and cursed place by the local Indians, who had a village up at Point Doughty and another below Freeman Island. The land in between these two villages was said to be home to a creepy critter called "He-Who-Eats," which was a thing that looked like a giant, hairless bear, only it was covered in mouths, like open sores all over its body . . . the mouths had sharp teeth, and when He-Who-Eats approached, you could hear the mouths gnashing in unison, "Eat . . . eat . . . eat!"

Another story that sticks out is the Grey Man, and that one always gave us the heebie-jeebies [Author's note: see the "Echoes of an Old Murder" chapter of this book]. *The way Jerry used to tell it, the Grey Man was a farmer in the 1800s who lost his mind on Halloween Night and started picking off the townsfolk one by one with a scythe, sort of like the Grim Reaper. He'd walk down the road with a red lantern and try every door along the way, and if it was unlocked, and they almost all were, he'd go in and murder everyone in the house. Now remember, our cabins we stayed in didn't have doors in those days!*

In the morning, the people who'd locked their doors went outside and found what had happened to their neighbors and a sheriff's posse was thrown together. They looked high and low for the Grey Man, but they never found him . . . and to this day, his ghost wanders the woods, holding out his red lantern in one hand and clutching his scythe in the other, its razor edge gleaming in the moonlight, still searching for anyone foolish enough to leave their door open in the night!

Now, it was around this point you'd hear something moving around in the forest, snapping twigs and rustling the bushes, and you'd start to catch glimpses of a red glow somewhere deep in the trees, a glow that seemed to be getting closer with each word of Jerry's tale!

Funnily enough, later on in our stay, I went to the

counselor's cabin to deliver a note, and I happened to see an old railroad lantern with a red globe sitting on the windowsill. I'm not sure I connected the dots at the time, but later on I had a good chuckle.

There were a few other stories, like one about a sailor's ghost who wanders around the north part of the camp, because his ship had been wrecked there a hundred years ago (a hundred years from any point in time, mind you). But those first two are the ones that really stick out in my mind.

Jim will be the first to admit that these stories were almost certainly invented by past counselors to frighten gullible youngsters and have little relation to historical fact—aside from the Grey Man's likely basis in the Olga murder of 1902. There is no known Swallah or Lummi myth corresponding to that of "He-Who-Eats," although this story bears a striking resemblance to certain native legends found in the remotest reaches of Vancouver Island. The stories, Jim says, exist to create memories that will last a lifetime, just as they have for him and for countless other alumni of Camp Orkila.

"I know things have changed a lot in the past fifty years," says Jim. "No more target practice, no more baseball or reveille, and last I heard they have doors on the cabins now."

Jim shakes his head and smiles. "But I just hope they're still scaring the kids."

A second tale, recalled by several older alumni,

involves the YMCA property at Twin Lakes. The ten-acre tract had been donated by Laurence Colman and the Robert Moran estate in 1947, for use as a more rustic and remote outpost for older campers. Tales were told of the old hermit Llewellyn Jenkins, whose squat and windswept farm had once sat above the cliffs near Raccoon Point. The counselors recounted how one camper had wandered away on a blustery night for one reason or another and had become hopelessly lost in the pitch-black woods—until he spied the lights of a lone cabin glowing somewhere up the coast. Making his way to the cabin and knocking, he was met by an old man with a long white beard, who said nothing, but gave the boy a compass and a flaming torch and silently sent him on his way. The boy shot his azimuth by torchlight and found his way back to the campsite—and when he returned, the counselors noted that his compass was of a very old type, tarnished green and more like something dug out of the ground—and, of course, no one could account for the mysterious cabin, other than to say it must have been the old Jenkins place . . . which, by then, had long since returned to nature.

In truth, a hermit of that name had indeed kept a farmstead on the wild coast beyond Buck Mountain. Llewellyn Jenkins, originally from St. Louis, Missouri, had served as a private in the 22nd Illinois Infantry during the Civil War. He lived the last years of his life on Orcas, and passed away there in 1913—undoubtedly having found a peaceful respite from the painful memories of the past. He is buried at Mount Baker Cemetery.

Other mysterious individuals, hermits of whom little else is known, once made their homes in the area. One recluse is known to have lived at the abandoned Estelle limeworks, on the present-day YMCA property at Moran. The old limeworks, built in the late 1880s, had been a sizable operation; the Seattle Lime Company had built wharves, ware-houses, housing, a short rail line, and a pair of kilns on the sheer cliffs, only for it all to be left deserted by the 1920s. Old-timers recalled rare sightings of the solitary dweller, and fires seen glowing in the moss-covered shacks on certain nights—and warnings to avoid the place, lest they be accosted by the deranged man. This story, too, likely influenced the ghostly tales told by latter-day YMCA campers.

* * *

Across the island, overlooking Victim Island on the shore of West Sound, sits the idyllic Camp Four Winds-Westward Ho, founded by Ms. Ruth Brown in 1927. Brown, who had been the executive director of the Camp Fire Girls in Seattle, had purchased an abandoned tract on the shore of West Sound after a lengthy search for a suitable location. The tract ran from an old homestead on the hill to a derelict salmon cannery that sagged on its pilings off Victim Island. With a great sense of vision, Ms. Brown set about redeveloping the land into what is today one of the finest youth camps in the Pacific Northwest.

Originally, Four Winds had been a girls-only camp; however, in 1935, Brown established Westward Ho, an adjacent camp for boys named for a sleek yawl of the same name—formerly the *White Wings II*, built by George Askew in the 1920s—that became the camp's official vessel.

Upon Ruth Brown's retirement in 1966, Camp Four Winds was donated to the Kaiser Family Foundation. The powerful Kaisers, of shipbuilding fame, had an estate called "the Carousel" which bordered Four Winds, and ensured that the camp would be well-stewarded into the present day.

Unlike Orkila, which has changed considerably since its inception, Four Winds has retained many of its old-fashioned traditions. Girls are still required to wear a uniform of middies and bloomers, and candlelight ceremonies are still held before the owl-flanked great lodge to mark the end of the season. Inside the lodge, campers have gathered at the stone hearth for generations to sing, play music, and tell stories—and on Lammas night, an ancient holiday marking the beginning of harvest, the stories take on a considerably spookier tone.

"Well, they told all kinds of stories you'd expect to hear at a summer camp," says Four Winds alumna and former kitchen manager Jess Ingram*.

"The kind-of-classic one they used to tell, that I

remember the most, was about how, way back before Orcas was settled by white people, there was a Native American village where the camp is today. They were a peaceful tribe, probably the Lummi I guess, but every year this other tribe from up north would come down and raid the village and take a few people away as slaves [...] never to be seen again. They'd always take kids, since I guess they made the best slaves, I don't know.

"Anyway, eventually the Lummi people in this village died off because of germs spread by the white people, and the village was abandoned, so there was no one there to kidnap for a long time. But then this white family homesteaded there and built a farm [...] and that year, the big canoes pulled up on the beach and they threw torches through the windows and killed everyone except the kids [...] they carried the kids off, and no one ever saw them again. The same thing would happen every time a new family tried to live there, even a long time after those northern tribes stopped raiding people. Every year a new family lived there, the kids would be carried off in middle of the night. And that kept happening after Four Winds was built. They'd always say that a kid named Bobby Higgins disappeared the season before [...] they found a big hole slashed in the tent and Bobby was gone, and no one ever saw him again [...] that used to scare everyone pretty good!"

Camp Orkila and Camp Four Winds are undoubtedly island institutions, and with hundreds of alumni newly-minted every year, who can say what spine-tingling tales may crop up in the coming decades?

Spirits from a Faraway Land

Are spirits bound by physical place, or can an artifact be just as haunted as a house? Sophie Walsh, an early historian of Orcas lore, set the stage for strange goings-on at the Deer Harbor home of Mr. John Laurence Walsh—no relation to Sophie—who had brought home a vast collection of weird artifacts and arcana from the far side of the Pacific . . . and with it, supposedly, a few full-fledged and hair-raising entities of the supernatural variety.

"The moon was shining on the water, the roads were strange and winding, leading up hill and down; the wind was in our ears as we dashed farther into the wilderness, till the only word that could express the sensation was 'shanghaied'," wrote Mrs. Walsh. The author was paying an evening visit to Mr. Walsh, who lived near Caldwell Point about a mile south of Deer Harbor.

Walsh was a Spanish-American War veteran, who for five years had tramped across the far Philippine Islands with his regiment; first fighting the ragged Spanish garrisons at Manila, and then removing to the southern islands of Mindanao, Jolo, and the Sulus, where a particularly bloody insurgency had arisen amongst the remote jungle tribes. He had returned in 1903 with the rank of sergeant, and a massive collection of "treasures such as cannot be found elsewhere," according to Mrs. Walsh. There was an eight-foot-long Moro "fiddle," or *kutiyapi*, and horn hammers, and tom-toms of beaten brass—and, more macabrely, battle-scarred shields and "terrible looking weapons"—which, to Sergeant Walsh, must have conjured nightmares of Army patrols deep in the unmapped jungles, and of opium-crazed tribesmen swarming down from the dark hills.

"One sleeps better if the true stories of these things are left untold," wrote Mrs. Walsh.

The veteran's collection was a source of fascination for visitors of all stripes, and many made the pilgrimage to Walsh's to view it and hear the veteran's wild stories. But soon enough, these visitors began to tell bizarre tales of their own, and rumors circulated that Walsh's place was haunted by some-thing that had come over with the collection—for these were no ordinary spooks . . .

Steve and Kathy Hodges* had purchased the old

Walsh place in the 1970s, and had every intention of making it an idyllic island getaway. But, according to Kathy, these plans were somewhat spoiled when the strange history of the house became apparent.

"Our neighbor, who was this nice old gentle- man who'd lived in Deer Harbor since probably the twenties, told us that our house was kind of 'notorious'," says Kathy. "We had no idea. People had heard a lot of odd things around there for years [...] babies crying at night, and someone whistling on the roads by the house [...] and a neighbor had seen a lady walking in our field, in a white dress, with long black hair, who was kind of glowing in the moonlight."

Inside the house, doors occasionally slammed of their own accord, and small objects appeared and reappeared—"[...] there was never anything really serious," says Kathy. But outside, they too heard the baby crying, and their daughter reported seeing a mysterious white figure outside her bedroom window.

"We were wondering what could possibly be going on [...] and after a while someone referred us to this Filipino gardener who worked at the Carousel, which was Edgar Kaiser's place," says Kathy.

The gardener was kind enough to stop by the Hodges's home, and after hearing the family's tales, informed them that they were being haunted by not one, but *two* distinct spirits—a *tiyanak*, a malevolent and demonic being taking the form of a newborn baby that cries in the woods—and an *engkanto*; a far more graceful spirit, often appearing as a "woman in white," who generally means no harm. These beings, said the gardener, could sometimes bind themselves to cursed objects and travel to new places, like young orb spiders drifting in the wind. Something in Walsh's collection had brought the things, and now that the collection was gone, the spirits had bound themselves to the house. It was unfortunate, he said, but such things were known to happen.

The Hodgeses no longer live at the old Walsh place, and much of the old soldier's collection has been scattered in the intervening years . . . though some pieces are now owned by the museum in Eastsound. As for the supposed spirits, who can say — few, if any, stories have surfaced recently of crying babies and women in white, leaving one to wonder how well the transplants have taken to life in this archipelago as opposed to the one they left.

Ghost Rock and Other Tales

An interesting little tidbit of island lore concerns the infamous "Witch Rock" or "Ghost Rock" occasionally referred to by early settlers. In his fascinating memoir, spanning from 1875 to 1910, Orcas pioneer James Francis Tulloch wrote that Ghost Rock was "[...] an immense white granite boulder which obtained its name from the Ignis Fatuus that was seen so often in this vicinity." He further elaborated:

This phosphorescent light evidently escaped from some fissure in the rocks and was only seen on still misty nights and mostly in the spring. We have on several occasions watched it from our windows. It would move slowly along near the ground for a time and resemble nothing so much as a lantern being carried by someone. Then, when moved by a gentle current of air, it would dart up a hundred feet or so and move around there.

It was little wonder that the place got its name of Ghost Rock. This so-called Jack-o-lantern or Will- o-the-wisp was quite common in Canada, but always seen along the near swamps where there was much decaying vegetation. But in this instance it was near the summit of a dry rocky hill and so was most unusual.

The lights had apparently been the cause of some amusement in the early days. According to Orcas pioneer Jack Geoghegan, "There was a story that a certain old-timer, when out fire-hunting for deer, had seen these strange lights one foggy night and, believing them to be a deer's eyes, had taken a couple of shots at them."

Tulloch's farm, Glenwood Springs—not to be confused with the Glenwood Inn at North Beach —is now home to a salmon hatchery, although aside from this it is largely unchanged from its 19th century appearance. The place had been odd from the start, it is said. Geoghegan recalled that a very ancient and overgrown road had been found on the mountain above the Tulloch place, and that no one knew who had built it or for what purpose . . . for it seemed to predate any road- building civilization in the islands. It bears mentioning, too, that the nearby beach at Tulloch's was said to have been the site of an Indian massacre in 1853, as mentioned in Tulloch's memoir:

My first farming was to dig up an area in front with a

mattock and plant it in potatoes. This ground was an old Indian village located here on account of the stream, the harbor and the clams.

One place was shown to me where 23 Indians were surprised and killed by one of the northern tribes. Those northern Indians were far more warlike than the Sound Indians whom they contemptuously called "Sap A Lalo" or bread eaters. I dug up many skeletons in this tract, one of which had the arrow head still in a rib.

Just offshore from the village site is Giffin Rocks, a pair of islets which were long known as a "depository for Indian dead," according to Fred John Splitstone's 1946 book.

"Here bodies were brought, wrapped in blankets, and placed in the boughs of the trees to remain until the elements had worn away flesh and wrappings, allowing the bones to fall to the ground," writes Splitstone. A gnarled juniper trunk, festooned with skulls, had lain across a southerly point of the rocks for many years, providing a profound shock to early boaters on the sound. In a macabre detail, Splitstone adds: "The last of these bones were carried away by souvenir hunters less than 20 years ago."

Tulloch had a few other odd stories to relate from his thirty-five years of living on Orcas. In the same memoir, he told of a large meteorite that plunged into the sound near his home, and of a hill by the Langdon Lime Works where a grove of trees had been struck by lightning a dozen or more times—possibly due to an unknown mineral in the rock—and also of experiencing a Fortean "frog fall" while delivering mail to Doe Bay:

On this day I was caught in a violent summer shower as I followed the trail along Cascade Lake and came suddenly on a space of about 100 yards in extent that literally was a moving mass of little green frogs about 1-½ inches in length. They were absolutely countless and simply covered the ground. While not one of the kind were to be seen elsewhere and under no circumstances could it be explained.

Another mysterious monolith mentioned by Tulloch was the "Devil-Devil Rock," a conical, ten-foot formation tucked along the eastern shore of East Sound just above Rosario. The rock had once featured prominently into Swallah lore; as Tulloch wrote, "[an] old Indian legend said it moved from place to place."

Indeed, according to early settler Luther Kimple, who had interviewed several aged Indians on the subject, the Devil-Devil Rock had been used to predict enemy raids with great accuracy.

"[Kimple] said they had quite a lot of faith in the rock," wrote W.R. Giffin in a 1935 history article. "They would watch the rock, and if the rock moved across the bay, they would either get ready for battle or take to hiding, for they knew that the Northern Indians were coming."

Giffin further noted:

There is one surviving pioneer lady living on the island that really believes in the "Devil-Devil" legend. She declared to me that when she was a young girl, she was coming up the bay one morning in her little canoe, and the rock was across the bay—and with almost the same breath she tried to convince me that she had not been drinking that morning, either!

There is another pioneer lady living on the Island, but who doesn't fancy having her name displayed in print, who gave me her idea about "Devil-Devil" rock. It sounds reasonable to me. She said that at extreme tide the rock is cut off from shore and forms a little bay behind the rock. She thinks that since the Indians travel with the tide, they would take advantage of high tides to come south on. When the native Indians would go down and see the rock cut off, they would expect the Northern Indians down. She thinks this was what the Indians meant when they said the "rock was across the bay." They meant the little bay that formed behind the rock.

In short, Tulloch and other early historians aptly demonstrate that, when it comes to weird phenomena on Orcas Island, there is truly nothing new under the sun.

At various times a haunt for smugglers, sightseers and seekers of spiritual enlightenment, the Inn is said to host a litany of ghosts, in addition to a mysterious "energy vortex" just offshore.
(University of Washington collection)

The old Augusta Mine on Mt. Constitution is said to be haunted by the miners who were entombed there in a freak cave-in . . .
(Fairhaven Pharmacy collection)

Capt. E. H. Smith, the "Hermit of Matia," settled on the little island off Orcas's northeast shore and became well-known for his psychic healing and telepathic powers. He vanished without a trace in 1921.
(Author's collection)

Passengers aboard the Waialeale *were shocked to sight a sea serpent gamboling in the waters near Orcas Landing in 1912.*
(F.J. Splitstone collection)

J.F. Tulloch's farm at the foot of Buck Mountain, where strange lights were seen dancing above the infamous "Ghost Rock," and where an Indian massacre occurred in the 1850s.
(Gordon Keith collection)

Harrison's dock and the old Madrona Inn are pictured to the left of Templin's dock, circa 1915. Madrona Point, an ancient burial ground, is said to be one of the most spiritually–active locales in Washington.
(University of Washington collection

The twin lakes and the twin islands—many strange sightings have occurred at Twin Lakes over the years, while the mysterious disappearances around Clark and Barnes Islands have led some to regard the area as Orcas's own "Devil's Triangle."
(University of Washington collection)

Despite its sleepy appearance, Olga was the site of much intrigue during the early part of the 20th century. Jack Hand was shot with a big-bore rifle on the Doe Bay road, while "Higgy," the monstrous bear, roamed the hills in search of prey.
(James T. Geoghegan collection)

The area around Point Doughty and the Glenwood Inn was said to have been a haven for smugglers and other criminals. A fortune in precious gems is supposedly buried there.
(James T. Geoghegan collection)

Prior to becoming a park, Mountain Lake was home to a community of hardscrabble farmers. Today, strange tales of sasquatch, ghosts, and silvery UFOs are whispered about the place.
(Orcas Island Historical Museum collection)

Camp Orkila, along with Camp Four Winds, have long been bastions of the classical "campfire tale" — with hair- raising yarns ranging from the horrifying "He-Who-Eats" to the ghostly hermit who helps lost campers. (Museum of History & Industry collection)

The Rosario estate is said to be haunted by the "Lady in Red," who barrels down nearby roads on a Harley-Davidson—while the mansion itself is supposedly so haunted that a séance there left a psychic catatonic. (Fred T. Darvill collection)

Port Langdon, a limeworks, was the first white settlement on the island. It was also the scene of the infamous Phillips murder, and a number of other shocking and bloody incidents.
(James T. Geoghegan collection)

The original Odd Fellows hall in Eastsound, circa 1914. Visitors have reported ghostly activity at the lodge for years, and some speculate that it may be the spirit of the ceremonial skeleton "Bonesy"—whose origins were never truly determined.
(James T. Geoghegan collection)

A traction engine and thresher of this type was said to have mangled a farmhand beyond recognition near Nordstrom's Lane in the early part of the 20th century. The veracity of this tale remains to be seen.
(Orcas Island Historical Museum collection)

Massacre Bay, Skull Island, and Victim Island are all clearly visible in this early photograph by Ferdinand Brady—as is the scene of the terrible Indian slaughter of 1858.
(Orcas Island Historical Museum collection)

The Orcas Hotel has greeted generations of visitors from its perch above the ferry landing. According to legend, the ghost of proprietress Octavia van Moorhem has stayed on to keep an eye on the place — and a phantom shootout still plays out on the front porch.
(F.J. Splitstone collection)

Diminutive Indian Island, once known as "Jap Island," was a focal point for bizarre talk of UFOs and Atlantean energy vortices amongst the New Age community.
(Orcas Island Historical Museum collection)

The 23-acre "Russian Settlement" was the single piece of property that could not be purchased for the state park. Landlocked on the summit of Mt. Constitution, the site now holds the radio towers.
(John B. Collins collection)

Mt. Constitution was known as Swelax *and considered a sacred site by the Swallah and Lummi tribes; it was the abode of Raven, a powerful and mysterious figure in Coast Salish mythology. To the New Agers, it was a hub of UFO activity, and said to contain a massive crystal.*
(James T. Geoghegan collection)

The Ghost Ship

The various straits and channels intersecting the San Juans make for rough seas, and when the nor'easters scream down from the Fraser River even the saltiest of seamen have been known to shudder in apprehension. Winds are magnified in the islands, sometimes enough to throw full- fledged ships onto the jagged rocks, and in the calm spells a thick fog shrouds the landmarks and makes traditional navigation nearly impossible—especially in those areas where magnetic disturbances send compass needles awry. For many seafarers, the islands have been a labyrinth from which there is no return.

Over the years, islanders have reported phantom ships in both East Sound and in the waters off North

Beach. Frank Worden* had two stories on the matter; in the first, on certain moonlit nights, a ghostly tall-ship could be seen gliding into Ship Bay and dropping anchor, while men in longboats rowed ashore and entered the woods with lanterns, engaged in some unknowable errand. The second tells of a mail steamer that struck Parker Reef during a night of foul weather in the early 1900s. No one knew of the wreck until the wee hours of morning, when witnesses on North Beach saw an old windjammer moving through a field of debris, picking up men from the water. Later that day, the island's mail washed ashore, and subsequently the news broke of its sinking. An aged mariner in town recognized descriptions of the wind-jammer as the *Jenny Mae*, which had foundered on Parker Reef some twenty years before. The old ship must have returned, he said, to retrieve the souls of the newly drowned crew.

Though Worden's yarn is just that, the Georgia Strait off Orcas was indeed the site of a deadly shipwreck. On May 18th, 1952, a thirty-six-foot sloop called the *Prelude* vanished with seven people aboard—Mr. and Mrs. Paul Fordyce were taking their young son Kenneth and two other couples, the Jukeses and the Cards, on a Sunday cruise to the San Juans, and were last sighted near the twin islands of Clark and Barnes at around five-thirty that afternoon. When the *Prelude* failed to put in at Bellingham, over one hundred vessels set out and combed the straits for the missing sightseers, but nothing turned up besides a few pieces of loose gear; no actual wreckage was ever recovered.

That Tuesday, four of the missing washed up on Lummi Island, and Mrs. Card's body was found on Blakely Island later that month. Mrs. Jukes and the yacht owner Paul Fordyce were never found. Speculation abounded as to what could have caused the disappearance, ranging from a catastrophic failure of the auxiliary engine to a rogue swell, but in the end the answer was known only to the dark and silent shore of Orcas Island.

Such disappearances were hardly unheard-of. The area around Clark and Barnes Islands has been the scene of several disappearances over the years—to the extent that some regard the place as Orcas's own "Devil's Triangle." In the 19th century, the smuggler "Pirate" Kelly is said to have drowned several smuggled Chinese in the narrow channel between the islands, and an island youth named Roy Reilly vanished there in the 1890s. Roy and his father had gone to Clark Island to build a raft, in order to tow home a number of livestock that had been pastured there. Unfortunately, the wind had picked up, and one of their boats had drifted away towards Orcas. Roy rowed out in pursuit and was never seen again.

In 1875, too, the sailing bark *Union*, an ex- whaler loaded with five-hundred-and-seventy- five tons of Nanaimo coal, grounded on a reef just feet from Clark Island. The crew survived, and insurance fraud was suspected; the first officer accused the captain of conspiring to collect the considerable payout. The matter went to trial, and in the end the captain was acquitted of all charges. Sea Scouts salvaged the *Union*'s anchor in 1969, and it currently serves as the mascot of Sehome High School in Bellingham.

In a much darker incident, a sixteen-foot motorboat and its four passengers went missing off Barnes Island in 1945. Coast Guard crews combed the straits, but only one body, that of Seattle resident Burgess Kern, was ever recovered.

More recently, a boater vanished northeast of the area in 1983, as did another in 1998, and a pair of kayakers in 2000. And in 2009, a forty-year-old Bellingham man vanished between Clark and Barnes Islands, while scuba diving in the deep channel where the Chinese had been drowned. 2009 had been a particularly dark year for Orcas, with a murder-suicide taking place there as well; a thirty nine-year old single mother had been strangled in her Sammamish apartment, and the murderer had taken her body to the San Juans aboard his powerboat. He killed himself in President Channel as law enforcement closed in.

Clark and Barnes Islands had been a notorious haunt of smugglers in the early days, so much so that Barnes Island had been called "Smuggler's" for much of its history. A gang had used the thirty-four-acre island as a hideout in the late 19th century, making use of the natural caves there to store rum and trafficked Chinese. A homesteader named Oscar Harte rediscovered the caves in 1915, and found rotted rum casks, a rusted gun barrel, and even deteriorated documents outlining the gang's operations. Later, Harte was told wild and bone-chilling tales of the gang's activities on the island by Joe Murakami, a Japanese fisherman who had squatted there in earlier days.

As for the supposed "Devil's Triangle," some local sailors point to the ferocious williwaw winds that sometimes shriek down from the summit of Mount Constitution. These sudden, swirling downdrafts have been known to capsize smaller boats in the area— perhaps lending further credence, too, to the Swallah's belief that Raven makes his nest atop *Swelax*.

* * *

On East Sound, many people have made claims of witnessing an ethereal vessel moving through the fog. It is usually described as a passenger steamer of the Mosquito Fleet-era, with some even identifying it as the *Clallam*, which went down in a gale south of San Juan in 1904, taking fifty-six souls to a watery grave.

"I saw the lights of a ship off my back porch," says Bruce Faulk*, whose home overlooks the sound from Mount Woolard.

"It was a clear night and there was a full moon, so you had pretty good visibility in all directions. I'm sitting out there, and clear as day there was a ship moving south from town there, all the windows lit up and everything. I'm thinking, 'is that a ferry?' because you don't typically see big boats down there, and this was about a two-hundred-footer, give or take. So I get up to grab my binoculars, for all of thirty seconds, and when I come back the ship is gone. Just *poof.* Like it was never there [...] I scanned the whole sound, up and down, as far as I could see, and there wasn't anything."

Bruce says he has asked neighbors about the strange ship, and at least one claimed to have seen a similar vessel in years past . . . although the neighbor made no mention of it vanishing.

"That had me shook up pretty good," says Bruce. "That's the kind of thing that makes you question your own sanity!"

La Conner resident Norm Ewing has a similar tale to tell. Norm and his wife Susie were taking their sailboat—a beautiful 1940s Senior Knockabout—on a quick cruise up to Eastsound when they were caught in a late-summer fogbank just south of Dolphin Bay.

"It's like pea soup," says Norm, ". . . it whites out everything around you, and all you can do is go off your instruments and hope everyone else is doing the same."

As the two motored up the sound, Norm operated their four-horsepower outboard while Susie navigated from inside the cabin. All was calm on the sound—the water was glassy, and even the chugging sound of the outboard was muffled by the fog. Norm was content to stare off into the white . . . that is, until he became aware of something out in the mist—something massive. And it was bearing down on them.

"Susie! *Radar!*" shouted Norm, but Susie seemed nonplussed.

"What are you talking about?" she replied. The radar screen showed nothing but open water ahead — nevertheless, Norm's eyes weren't deceiving him, and he slammed the tiller starboard and clear of the thing's path. He said nothing as the shape drew closer, and the details became discernable . . . it was a ship, an old one, with a black wooden hull and rows of dark windows along its white upper deck. A smokestack rose up high behind the pilothouse but there was no smoke to be seen.

Norm called out "Ahoy there!" as they passed, but no reply was given. He searched the windows for signs of life and thought he saw shadowy figures behind the glass, but there was no light inside and it was difficult to tell. He also made note of the ship's name, painted on the bow: CLALLAM.

The ship passed by, and Norm watched as it faded back into the fog. It was only after the ship had gone that he realized two things—the *Clallam* had made no sound, and it left no wake . . .

A final variation of the tale: a married couple, Paul and Nancy Gardner*, were Christmas shopping for their grandchildren at Darvill's Bookstore some years ago when Paul happened to spy something out the window. It was nearing dusk and lightly snowing, but Paul saw clearly a steamship of the old variety, sitting alongside the wharf on Madrona Point with no signs of life. Of course, at the turn of the century there had been a dock extending out from the rocky point, where a freight depot was built and passengers unloaded, but it had all been torn down years before. Paul turned to alert his wife, but when he looked back the ship and its berthing were gone. Nancy did not personally view the spectral ship, but did make note of her husband's demeanor at the time. "He saw something," she says.

It comes as no surprise that Orcas, a piece of land surrounded by saltwater, should boast a number of spooky maritime legends. How could it not, when the fogbanks roll in and the grey winter seas begin to crash on deserted beaches?

The Kilns

The old limekilns of Orcas Island sit in seclusion now, their ivy-choked stone walls looming through the trees at remote points like the watchtowers of some forgotten kingdom. But these kilns were once the heart of a thriving industry, and their product built the modern cities of the West Coast. And at the old Langdon Lime Works, south of Eastsound, a number of spine- tingling legends were born that have endured to the present day.

A few miles away, on the eastern shore of East Sound, sits the ancient Langdon Lime Works, where the elaborate stone ruins have melded into the hillside and grown over with moss and cedar sprouts and English ivy. The small bay below Coon Hollow, unnamed on nautical charts, had been a notable locale in Lummi lore; it was the site where the first deer was created, out of the primordial aether of the spirit world. Later, limestone outcroppings on the hillside attracted the eye of passing settlers, and a limeworks was erected. "Port Langdon," established by George R. Shotter in 1862, had been the first such outpost on Orcas Island, and had employed many of the early settlers as woodcutters and quarrymen; there were also less savory characters at the kilns, men who James F. Tulloch called "sailor scum" in his famed memoir. One of these less-than-upstanding citizens was a Welsh cooper named George Phillips, who had married Xwelas, the former wife of Edmund Clare Fitzhugh (see the "Haunted Hotels" chapter of this book). Xwelas, now in her forties, had been born into Samish-Clallam nobility, but was now the wife of a common—and by all accounts, brutish—laborer.

One incident, which likely gives an accurate picture of their relationship, was recounted by Tulloch. "I had witnessed some trouble between Phillips and his squaw [...] while they were passing my place in their canoe," writes Tulloch, whose farm was situated near Port Langdon and the Phillips cabin. "The quarrel ended by the squaw striking him on the head with a paddle and it was no love tap either."

Their marriage had already been marred by a tragic incident which took place at the lime works in 1877. Their two small children had found their way into a storeroom and dropped a lighted match into a can of black powder, "[...] causing them both a horrible death from inhaling the flames."

The following year, their rocky relations would finally come to a head. Here two variations of the incident emerge; in the first, told by Xwelas herself, the couple had come to a particularly violent altercation while paddling home from a night of drinking and gambling at a neighbor's. Phillips had attacked the pregnant Xwelas with an oar and threatened to kill her. Upon arriving home, he told Xwelas to pack her things and leave, and began loading his firearm. Her son, Mason Fitzhugh, tried to mediate, but Xwelas decided it was best to spend the night in the forest. She strapped her infant daughter Maggie to her back, took a loaded shotgun, and left.

The next morning, Christmas Day, Phillips and Fitzhugh went out looking for Xwelas and the child. The mother and daughter had concealed themselves behind a boulder near the Port Langdon well, and as Phillips and Fitzhugh approached, Baby Maggie cried out and gave away the hiding spot—and Xwelas leapt up and gave her husband both barrels. As one local newspaper quipped, "Indian women are not to be trifled with."

The second version, related by Tulloch, is thus:

It developed that Phillips wanted his stepson Mason Fitzhugh, who was the son of Fitzhugh of Whatcom, who tried and acquitted himself of murder, to marry a sister of Joseph Bull, but the squaw with a natural jealousy of her race, thought that Phillips was like John Alden, speaking for himself [Author's note: a reference to Longfellow's *The Court-ship of Miles Standish*], *and lay for him with a shotgun, both charges entering his neck and breast and causing almost instant death.*

Xwelas, indicted for murder, spent many months in the jail at Port Townsend awaiting trial. She gave birth to her son Thomas there in February of 1879, and that September was finally handed a verdict: manslaughter. Cleared of a murder charge, Xwelas was sentenced to two years of hard labor, with ten months already served, and lived out the remainder of her life in relative anonymity on the Lummi reservation. She would make newsprint for a final time in August of 1883—according to the article, Xwelas had found a barrel of stolen mail stashed near the mouth of the Nooksack River and alerted the local post- master. She passed away near the place of her birth in 1918.

The days of blood at Port Langdon were far from over, however. In November of 1907, two workmen were killed in a powder explosion at the quarry— superintendent Chris Johnson, forty-two, and Fred Baatz, a youth of seventeen from Waldron Island. As the *San Juan Islander* later reported:

The two men were alone, preparing to "shoot" two holes which had been drilled in the top of a ledge of lime rock about 120 feet above the bay, from the shore of which the cliff rises precipitously. A few moments before the accident Mr. Johnson had called down to Foreman Philip [Peter Philip, no relation to George] *to send up a piece of fuse and a cap and one of the men had just started up with them, with the aid of a rope which hung over the face of the cliff, when there was a terrific explosion and the startled men below hurried to shelter themselves from the rocks which they knew would soon be coming down. Mr. Philip says that he glanced upward as he ran to a place of safety under the cliff and could see the body of Mr. Johnson high in the air amidst masses of rock discharged by the blast. The body came down over the most jagged portion of the cliff, striking the ground right at the water's edge. The right arm was blown off and was not found; the left was broken and terribly lacerated; the eyes were gone and the head and body most terribly mangled. The body of young Baatz was found a short distance away from that of Mr. John- son and a little up the hillside. It was also horribly mangled, though no limbs were gone.*

Answers were searched for but none were found. As the article stated, "Just how the accident occurred will never be known." It was simply another mysterious footnote in the dark history of Port Langdon.

These events, in turn, have led to numerous frightening legends. Stories tell of ghostly fires seen glowing in the old kiln and of an eyeless specter wandering below the cliffs—and of phantom shotgun blasts echoing down from the hillside where the Phillips murder took place. One old-timer, Bud Powers*, had a chilling encounter there in the early 1960s, when the workings were owned by the Crown Zellerbach Corporation. The company had hired Bud as a caretaker, and he would stop by periodically to make sure the place was in order.

"[Crown Zellerbach] used to quarry 'paper rock' out of there, for their pulp mill, but it'd been closed for a few years. It wasn't anything they cared much about, but they hired me on to look after the place and make sure nobody was dumping their trash in the old quarry," said Bud. "It was a hell of a place to get to in those days. You'd go down the private road there and then you'd have to go onto an old logging spur, and that was all overgrown like a jungle [...] and from there I'd have to go on foot."

One particularly cold and blustery morning, Bud went to make his daily rounds at the old limeworks. He parked his truck at the end of the logging road and skirted down through the woods, picking his way through the salal and gooseberry, until he came to the kilns.

"I poked around that way for a few minutes and enjoyed the view," said Bud. He found shelter just inside the kiln's drawhole as a light rain began to fall, and watched the wind whip up whitecaps and long rollers on the sound that swelled high and broke against the nearby rocks. He was enjoying the solitude—until he heard something hair-raising over the wind.

"It was a child's laugh," said Bud. Indeed, the distinct sound of children's laughter could be heard over the rising wind—a wind that, to Bud, seemed to be getting colder by the second. Filled with a deepening sense of dread, as no children should have at play at such a place, especially when the day was stormy and school was in session, Bud decided to high-tail it back to his truck; with the old campfire tales of eyeless specters and violent deaths and Indian legends perhaps playing more of a part than he was willing to admit. As he crashed through the heavy underbrush, he swore that the laughter was following him, and rapidly becoming more and more demented as it cackled through the misty trees . . . finally, he reached his truck and reversed wildly down the deeply rutted spur until he was well clear of the accursed kilns. Bud, sufficiently spooked, filed his two-weeks' notice with Crown Zellerbach and has never returned to the old Langdon Lime Works.

The old Gregg kiln at Judd Cove is also said to be haunted. Built by Captain Nathan Gregg in 1888, on what was then called Desperate Harbor, it operated until around 1902 when the limestone deposit was finally exhausted. Left to crumble for many years, it was only recently purchased by the San Juan County Land Bank and restored to its former appearance.

One sightseer, Allie Brooks*, reported a rather startling encounter—already feeling a "weird energy," she had gone to look inside a fenced passageway in the kiln and was instead confronted by the grey, transparent figure of a man, who disappeared a split-second later. Much like Bud Powers's tale, Allie reported feelings of being watched as she made her way back to the parking lot. Interestingly, no deaths are known to have occurred at the Judd Cove kiln, and Allie's is the only known account of ghostly activity there.

The Gregg kiln is open to the public, as part of the Land Bank's Judd Cove Preserve, whereas the old Langdon Lime Works is private and not open for visitation—as, perhaps, is best for all concerned.

Ghosts of the North Shore

Odd occurrences have long been a mainstay of Orcas Island's north shore—the dark and pebbly strand running from Point Doughty to the dramatic formations around Terrill Beach and Point Thompson, where Nanaimo bedrock juts out in tremendous crags and ripples down into the sea like cooled magma. Such locations lend themselves to ghostly tales, as storytellers like Frank Worden* were so acutely aware, and so we naturally find North Beach and the surrounding coast as the setting for the following tales—historical or otherwise.

A favorite tale of Worden's was that of the bloody and horrific apparition said to wander the beach on foggy days and dark evenings . . . he would tell it often during his bonfire recitals, always making sure that the audience knew they were sitting *on that very beach* . . .

George Hall Richardson was one of the early settlers of Whatcom, who had deserted from the HMS *Satellite* in Victoria and made his way into American territory at the close of the Pig War. Richardson soon dropped his last name, and as George Hall taught at the first schoolhouse on Bellingham Bay, located near the Sehome coal mine. Later, he would work as a collier at the mine.

On June 30th, 1871, while paddling back from Cowichan, British Columbia with his Samish wife Fanny and her sister, Richardson spotted a deer grazing somewhere along the northern shore and jumped from the canoe with his pistol in order to have a shot at it. In doing so, however, he stumbled on a rock and inadvertently tripped the pistol's hammer, discharging it into his abdomen. As reported in the *Olympia Transcript* of July 15th, "He died soon after."

Worden's lurid take on the tragedy was this: that, when the conditions were suitably spooky, the specter of George Richardson would stumble out of the fog, clutching his oozing stomach, and shamble towards you in all his blood-soaked horror, moaning "HELP ME . . . *HELP ME!*"

On other nights, Worden would tell a similar tale, though the identity of the shambling specter was changed to that of Skookum Tom, a mysterious figure whose doings were whispered of with breathless terror in the early days of the San Juans. Tom, or

Clackia, was an Indian from Kuper Island, British Columbia who was suspected of at least three murders in the area—including that of William O'Donnell on Orcas—and was known to hide out on Matia Island. His name appears with devilish regularity in old accounts, even in a slightly removed capacity; the ill-rumored Lars Brown had implicated Tom in the Yves J'Affret murder. Most shockingly, he had been named as the mastermind of a particularly brutal attack on a group of Bella Bella Indians at Porlier Pass, in the Gulf Islands, in 1877. At Tom's urging, it was said, a party of five Penelakut had overtaken the Bella Bella canoe and forced the seven occupants ashore—women and a child among them—where they were mutilated, shot, and burned on the beach, in what the *Victoria Standard* called "one of the most repugnant crimes ever committed by the Indians."

Tom was also known to associate with "Colonel" Enoch May, the island's arch-criminal, who lived between North Beach and the present-day OPALCO plant. "[Here] he had a band of the worst Indian characters always camped under the leadership of an outlaw Indian known as Old Tom, to whose credit more than one murder was attributed," wrote James F. Tulloch, another early settler.

Skookum Tom never answered for his crimes, and his spirit, said Worden, could be seen on moonless nights stalking the beaches with a long and blood-rusted knife, forever drawn to the sight of campfires blazing along the lonely shore . . .

Worden was also quick to mention the ghostly red cross seen glowing on the rocks at North Beach on nights preceding a big squall. Seasoned sailors knew what the cross meant, though they did not know what it was or how it came to be—they simply knew to turn back or find shelter at Fossil Bay. Surely enough, there had been a mysterious cross at North Beach in the early days—according to a travelogue from 1903, "[...] a large red cross used to be seen painted upon the rocks, which, since the going of the red men, has disappeared."

Worden drew connections between the cross and the earliest Spanish explorers who gave Orcas its name—*horcas*, in the Spanish language, means "gallows." The Spaniards had supposedly hanged a mutinous crewman on the island and named it accordingly. Naturally, this contradicts the more widely accepted version, that "Orcas" derives from *Horcasitas*; the name of the viceroy who had chartered the expedition.

Another spirit said to haunt the north shore is that of an old Indian woman seen drifting along the beach by Smuggler's Villa Resort and Brandt's Landing (see the "Haunted Hotels" chapter of this book). She is sometimes described as "stooped" and carrying a cedar basket.

Closer to Point Doughty and the old Glenwood Inn, reports have surfaced of whispers in the fog and strange shadows that dart through the trees—supposedly the spirits of Chinese laborers smuggled in from Canada by notorious figures such as Lawrence Kelly, Victor McConnell, and "Colonel" Enoch May. These smugglers would stash their human cargo along the remote shoreline to avoid revenue cutters, sometimes abandoning them to the elements when a return trip could not be made. At least one smuggler was reported to have kept his passengers bound up in weighted burlap sacks; so that, if a revenuer threatened to overtake them, the human evidence could be disposed of quickly and without a fight. "Pirate" Kelly is alleged to have thrown several of these unfortunates into the deep channel between Clark and Barnes Islands in the late 19th century.

"Everyone usually figured that stretch of beach past Gibson's was haunted," said Betty Wallace, who had summered on Orcas since the late 1930s. "[...] Colonel May and his lot used to hide Chinese and opium in the forest up that way. Him and Skookum Tom had an outlaw camp at Onaway Beach for that kind of thing [...] the rumor was there were a few Chinese buried out there. I never saw much, but Dick [Betty's brother] and I saw a shadow there once, moving very fast in the trees. But then it might have been a deer—except there was no sound of it running away."

As one newspaperman of the period waxed, "[...] how many spooks of drowned Celestials nightly visit the couch of the Smuggler, their pigtails wet and slimy with the ooze of the caverns of the sea?"

Orcas Island, to the surprise of some, was a haunt

for characters of ill-repute even in the very early days. In the 1860s, a trio of outlaws from the Idaho Territory, said to be responsible for a string of murders and stage-robberies near Fort Hall, had escaped to British Columbia, where they were subsequently detained by the local authorities. Lawmen from Boise City were dispatched to bring the men home, but upon arriving found that, due to a delay in the paperwork, their quarry had been prematurely released.

The trio, consisting of George Smith, "Brocky Jack" Dulligan, and a man named Murphy, had departed for the San Juans, and the Idaho lawmen chartered an armed schooner to hunt them down. Eventually the outlaws were cornered at their hideout on Orcas Island and taken into custody—"Brocky Jack" and company had been mounting "plundering expeditions" for some time since their initial escape, and a large amount of stolen property was recovered. The precise location of their hideout, unfortunately, has been lost to time . . . although the alleged "robber's roost" at North Beach presents a compelling possibility. Henry Wagner, better known as "The Flying Dutchman," was rumored to use the area for similar operations some forty years later (see the "Lost Treasures" chapter of this book).

Human remains in various states of decay have been found in the area for years, perhaps further adding to the north shore's dark mystique. Chinese bodies were recovered around Sucia Island, once a notorious smuggler's haven itself, and an unidentified man's body is known to have washed ashore at Raccoon Point in 1906. The body, eaten away beyond recognition, had been found floating in the luminescent kelp-beds so long shunned by the superstitious natives. At the direction of coroner George Wright, a pyre of driftwood and brush was heaped together on the beach, and the body hurled on as spectators gathered and looked on from the banks and tree branches and various other vantage points.

The body of one Philip Wenzel, also, was found by hunters near Point Lawrence in 1896, in the same area where a footless skeleton was found in 2007, causing some to speculate on its connection to the tennis shoe-clad feet found elsewhere in the Puget Sound and Canada. And in 2009, in a strange echo of past deeds, a badly decomposed body was found afloat near Sucia, draped on the rocks of Parker Reef.

Further west on Orcas, at Point Doughty, a man called John Paul George, or simply "Indian George," made his home for many years with a woman named Martha, who was variously described as his wife or daughter. George was the last keeper of the ancient reefnet at Point Doughty, called *Tlqwoloqs* in the Lummi dialect, a place that had been fished for thousands of years—the last of a long line, since his kinsman Patrick George had fallen to his death from the bluffs in 1909. John Paul was a beloved figure, and summer visitors fondly recalled him bringing gifts of salmon and teaching youngsters the value of medicinal plants. Though George's cabin and smokehouse are long gone, many—including the YMCA campers who frequent the point—have reported feeling a benign presence watching over them as they explore the sawtooth cliffs and wind-sculpted firs; perhaps a reminder of the gentle fisherman and his companion who once called the place home.

Haunted Eastsound

According to the ancient beliefs of certain Northwestern tribes, "spirit paths" are other-worldly avenues which crisscross the landscape in straight lines, and are traveled at night by the dead and other beings; one such spirit path purportedly cuts straight through the heart of Eastsound, and some allege that this would account for the town's reputation as one of the more haunted locales in Washington state.

April's Grove, for one, a relatively recent housing development on the edge of Eastsound, is located along the path. Named for a beloved brown cow who once grazed in the adjacent field, April's Grove was built by the OPAL Community Land Trust as affordable housing in 2019. The land itself had been vacant for many years, but was formerly occupied by the old McGlinn place. The fire department had burned the house as a training exercise, and many locals were reportedly glad to see the place go; it had garnered something of a "bad rep" in later years, although how that reputation was earned is some-thing the old-timers are generally unwilling to discuss.

In the scant few years since opening, April's Grove has already become the source for at least one odd accounts. Kat Wachsmuth, a resident for only three months, wrote in an email correspondence with the author:

I had a very interesting experience living there. As a Wiccan, I am naturally sensitive to emotions, auras, and spirits. When I first came to April's Grove my whole body started vibrating as soon as I drove up. I knew right away that this was a very spiritually active place, and that living here was going to be "interesting." But I didn't have a choice because I was going through a lot at the time and I didn't have anywhere else to stay [...] because my mom was being a [expletive]. *There were a lot of really toxic people in my life and that might have made me more sensitive at the time, too. My new neighbor Jillian* was really welcoming though, and we bonded because we'd both been through a lot of trauma and abuse. I told her that I'm sensitive and she warned me that my building was already kind of notorious even though it was only a year old. That was worrying for me but I didn't have a choice.*

The first experience I had was literally the night I moved in. I felt the temperature drop in my bedroom to the point where I could see my breath. This happened in June, by the way. Then

I saw a black shadow materialize in the corner for maybe three seconds, kind of like smoke. I saw spirits constantly after that. There was the black shadow that always made the room cold and brought a negative energy, and a Native American woman who brushed her hair by the window. And there was a little boy dressed in old fashion clothes. Once I saw a woman in white pass by my window, but I lived on the second floor.

I think that most of the ghosts are Native American spirits who are angry that April's Grove was built on their land. And a few are from the old house that used to be there. Jillian told me that she felt a strong energy at one spot by a huge madrona tree, and she sensed there were at least three child skeletons buried there.

Just down the road, reports of ghostly Indians seen walking the streets of Eastsound have circulated for years. Ghost hunter Randall Maier, who had earlier investigated the Orcas Hotel, spoke of his experiences there:

"[...] we walked around Eastsound for a few hours, from about midnight to four in the morning, on a kind of damp, foggy night. We had the whole town to ourselves so we got some pretty decent readings [...] our EMF [Electromagnetic Field] reader started going crazy on the main street by Ray's Pharmacy, and Alex got some really amazing photos around there, of some orbs, some streaks, and even what looks like a full-bodied apparition.

"[Our friend] Maddie had the craziest experience,

though. She actually physically saw an apparition. It was in the park by the waterfront, towards the end of the night [...] actually, it might have even been the witching hour. She said it was a Native American woman, dressed in traditional clothes, carrying a basket. When [Maddie] tried to get our attention, the woman disappeared before any of us could see it. Not that we could have, probably, because she's very much sensitive, and she sees things the rest of us don't."

The native history of Eastsound, naturally, can be traced back many thousands of years. A village called *Tsel Whi'sen* existed at Madrona Point, and at least two massacres are known to have occurred in the area— one at Crescent Beach, an area once noted for its abundance of artifacts, and another at the Glenwood Springs farm, where at least twenty-three Indians were said to have been killed, and hundreds more wounded or taken prisoner by the Stikine. A number of skeletons found buried in shell middens at Crescent Beach are currently housed at the Burke Museum in Seattle—and a lone woman rests beneath Main Street outside the Outlook Inn.

Early Eastsound was the scene of strange doings in the days of white settlement, as well. In 1882 a man named Charles Emerson was found dead amidst a bizarre and ghastly scene in his cabin, which sat in the vicinity of Charles Shattuck's original store. Though reportedly "a man of some ability, and well educated," he was also a former inmate of the Steilacoom insane asylum—and his behavior had noticeably worsened leading up to the incident. One day, Shattuck went to check on the afflicted man—and was horrified by what he found.

"The body presented a most horrible appearance, being partially devoured by hogs or other animals," wrote the *Northwest Enterprise*. Emerson had barricaded the cabin and destroyed any books or papers which might have revealed his personal history or motive for suicide. He then attached a string to the trigger of his firearm and shot himself through the heart.

Incidentally, another grisly incident had occurred on the very site of Emerson's suicide just four years earlier—there was "a sort of fatality about the place," said the paper. A man named William O'Donnell had occupied the spot, and had been found there, shot in the chest and buried beneath a pile of fence rails and underbrush. Though no arrest was made, the shadowy Skookum Tom was suspected.

The Lower Tavern, an Eastsound mainstay, is purportedly another hotspot of paranormal activity. A former line cook at the Lower described a variety of strange phenomena:

"We'd stack all the chairs when we closed up for the night, and sometimes we'd come in in the morning and find them all unstacked [...] there was other stuff, too, like there were these cold spots that people would complain about [...] this one time a table called one of the staff over and they were complaining about how cold it was, could we turn up the heat, blah, blah blah [...] well, according to the thermostat it was already pretty warm in there, so she didn't know what they were talking about, until she leaned in a little closer and felt it [...] for some reason, the air around this one table actually was so cold you could almost see your breath."

Customers and employees alike have also reported disembodied voices, phantom footsteps, and doors opening and closing of their own accord, so much so that employees have taken to calling the spook "Gramps," after an old regular who passed away many years ago.

"I'm not sure if anyone knew Gramps's real name," says one of the waitstaff, "but he used to plant himself at that bar for five or six hours almost every day, for ten or fifteen years [...] there's some weird stuff that happens in here, for sure, but to me it never feels mean or anything. I think it's just old Gramps, still hanging out."

Others attribute this phenomenon to the building's past as a medical center—the building on Prune Alley had been constructed as the Orcas Island Medical Clinic in the early 1970s, a significant change from the "country doctor" care of earlier days. The clinic operated there until the larger facility on Deye

Lane opened in 1992. Of course, during the future tavern's time as a medical center, a number of deaths occurred, and some believe these to be the cause of the Lower's current manifestations.

The old Methodist manse at 65 North Beach Road, adjoining the present-day bakery on the intersection with Main Street, was built in the late 1880s to house the minister of the since-demolished Methodist church. As of this writing, the manse hosts both an upscale boutique and the offices of the Orcas Island Chamber of Commerce, along with a rather spooky collection of eerie tales.

A woman in a white dress has supposedly been seen sitting at the upstairs window overlooking the street, even at times when the manse was vacant or undergoing renovation. Usually described as having a sad expression, she vanishes if scrutinized for too long. A former tenant, real estate agent Robyn Young*, reported hearing muffled voices and footsteps coming from the empty second floor, including what sounded like an argument between a man and a woman, and once saw a pull chain from a light fixture sway wildly despite there being no breeze.

Situated alongside the Orcas Island Historical Museum is the Our House Mall, an annex which houses several retail shops and restaurants. Attached and somewhat hidden at the rear of this relatively new structure is the old Our House building, one of the most historic locations in Eastsound. Originally constructed as a one-room schoolhouse in 1888, it was remodeled extensively in the 1890s and was eventually replaced by the much larger school on Stroud's Hill in 1904—itself superseded by the Nellie S. Milton building in 1949. The disused school was purchased by a real estate broker and subsequently converted into a boarding house known as "Our House," a title that has endured into the present day, even after its rooming days have long since passed. More recently it has served as a restaurant.

Unsurprisingly, this storied structure is said to be haunted. According to Shawna Linscott, who worked at a now-defunct café in Our House, silverware would fly off the tables and pots and pans would rattle in the empty kitchen.

"We'd always get complaints that someone was smoking," says Shawna. "And there was never anyone. I smelled it a few times, too. It was cigar smoke, and there was never anyone smoking a cigar."

Shawna also mentioned having her hair pulled, and hearing what sounded like a man clearing his throat almost directly behind her—despite the place being deserted. Some point to the building's past as a boarding house in order to explain this frightening phenomenon; a traveling salesman is said to have committed suicide there in the early 1930s, although the author has found no newspaper accounts to corroborate this. Others have theorized that the spirit may be that of "Buckskin" Frank Leslie, a gambler, gunfighter, and former cavalry scout who had been a rather notorious figure in Tombstone, Arizona during its heyday. Leslie was also a convicted murderer and conman who had served several years at Yuma for the killing of his common-law wife. In March of 1912, Leslie filed for a homestead on the ragged coast below Sea Acres and allegedly boarded at Our House for nearly two years, during which time he was legally obligated to cultivate or otherwise improve the land. He did nothing of the kind, and by 1914 his claim had been contested and canceled. Leslie left the island, never to return.

Established in 1960, the Sea View Theater represented a major leap forward for the island community. It was one of the first truly modern businesses on Orcas, featuring the latest movies and sporting features such as a soda fountain and pop-corn machine. Despite the island's small population, the theater never suffered from lack of business.

A wide variety of eerie happenings have been reported by staff and movie-goers alike over the years. Kirsten Whipple*, who worked at the Sea View periodically in the mid-2000s, mentioned talk of "cold spots" in a few locations around the theater, strange voices, and the ubiquitous flickering lights. Kirsten also mentioned a ghostly and oppressive "presence" in the projector booth.

According to theater employees, in addition to this presence, a shadowy figure has been reported looming in the window by the marquee. Kirsten did not personally view this phenomenon but noted that a number of her friends and co-workers had.

The old Porter's Garage building, currently home to the Madrona Bar & Grill, was built in 1938 as a Standard Oil filling station, repair shop, and Dodge-Plymouth dealer, and later served as an earlier iteration of the Lower Tavern called the Old Gaffer's Pub. With its striking view of the sound and rustic charm, the building has been a popular venue for many decades—and with this popularity has come a handful of ghostly tales.

Jeremy Evans, one of the contractors who helped renovate the building in 2009, discussed his crew's many unusual experiences in the old garage:

"Let's see, we'd have tools go missing all the time [...] I thought someone had took my Sawzall, but then it showed up the next morning in a completely different spot [...] one of our guys couldn't find his speed square, but a couple of days later we found it on top of one of the rafters. No idea how it got there.

"One guy almost quit because he felt something pull on his [tool] belt. Obviously there was no one there and he got pretty freaked out. He ended up staying on but he would absolutely refuse to be in there alone."

Eastsound, with a history dating back thou- sands of years to the earliest Indian settlement, is a place that few others can rival in terms of both quaint charm and unearthly reputation. Though times have certainly changed, and despite the creeping specter of modernization, elements of the past seem to linger on in Eastsound, the "Vacation Land Complete."

Ghosts of Madrona Point

Madrona Point, it would seem, is one of the more spiritually-active locales on Orcas Island. Jutting out dramatically from the head of East Sound, some have referred to the thirty-three-acre peninsula as the "heart of the island"—a title that is none too exagg-erated, considering its six thousand-year-history. The Swallah and Lummi tribes had a village called *Tsel Whi'sen* there and considered the place a spiritual equal of *Swelax*, or Mount Constitution, the abode of the Raven god. Medicinal plants grew in abundance at *Tsel Whi'sen*, and the dead were susp-ended high in the trees and in burial middens dating back to the Paleo-indian Period.

The early white settlers followed suit, and a small "burying ground" was established at Madrona Point, which was mostly populated by Indians and the mixed children of Hudson's Bay men. By the late 1880s the need for a more developed cemetery was becoming clear, and so the Orcas Island Cemetery Association was formed, with the principals being Michael Adams, John N. Fry, and James F. Tulloch, who was appoint-ted chairman of the board. The Association attempted to purchase the point from the government, but a snag was soon encountered; the government could not sell the land to an organization, but only to private citizens. As a loophole, the trustees agreed to purchase the land jointly in their own names and afterward deed the land to the Association.

This they did, but soon another issue emerged; Sidney R.S. Gray, the influential Episcopal rector, wished to reinter the dead at a different site that was farther inland—the future Mount Baker Cemetery. Tulloch opposed the logistics of this and called for a vote on the issue. As it happened, however, Tulloch's steamer broke down in Seattle on the day before the vote—and upon his return, he found that Adams and Fry had elected to sell the land to none-other than Elder Gray and the Harrison brothers, Eb and Isaac.

A lengthy legal battle ensued, but in the end Madrona Point came fully under the ownership of Dr. Isaac M. Harrison and his wife, Agnes. The Harrisons were both practicing physicians, and Dr. Agnes Barlow Harrison became a particularly well-known and beloved figure in the San Juans, delivering over two-thousand infants by the end of her career. At

Madrona Point, the Harrisons constructed a wharf for the Mosquito Fleet steamers and a twenty-four-cottage resort called the Madrona Inn. The Inn operated for over fifty years, but, much like the old boneyard, few traces remain today.

Norton Clapp, the chairman of the Weyerhaeuser Corporation and former owner of Turtleback Mountain, purchased Madrona Point in 1967. The site was quiet until the late 1980s, when excavators suddenly appeared along Haven Road and the news broke of Clapp's intention to bulldoze the point for condominiums. The tycoon was foiled by local activists, however; New Agers had banded together with historians to save the site.

Not all were pleased with this unusual union, especially when the spiritualists organized a pagan "prayer vigil" at the point.

"Several longtime residents refused to go because they heard the group intended to use Indian drums and bird feathers to commune with the property's past and future souls," wrote one reporter. Others were disturbed that the New Agers had released a "Spiritual Impact Statement" warning that the spirits of Madrona Point would be "offended" if the development were to take place.

Nevertheless, through the efforts of these activists, a hefty appropriations bill was passed that purchased Madrona Point in trust for the Lummi Nation. In 2007, citing vandalism, the Lummi closed off access to the point, and for many years a hand-painted sign stood reading, "SACRED GROUND, LEAVE NOW." It remains closed as of this writing.

Since being sealed to visitors, Madrona Point has mostly returned to its natural state—and its rather spooky reputation as a burial ground has influenced a number of legends about the site. According to Dave Redfield*, a lifelong islander, Norton Clapp had brought in a small crew of Weyerhaeuser men to clear out some of the more ancient and corpse-fed firs on the point. The loggers were only able to fell a few before they uncovered a skeleton caught up in the roots of a fallen fir. Afterward, everything went horribly wrong—equipment malfunctioned, choker cables snapped, and one man was nearly killed by "barberchair" snag that split vertically and fell in the wrong direction. And soon enough, even stranger occurrences began; the men reported hearing drums and a faint and rhythmic chanting coming from everywhere and nowhere at once. Eventually, the phenomena became so frightening that the loggers packed up and fled, leaving behind a stack of logs that, to this day, have never been bucked or hauled away. This resistance—supernatural or otherwise— was a key factor in Clapp's decision to sell the point, says Redfield.

An old house on the point, dating from the Madrona Inn-era, is said to be haunted by tiny, multi-colored orbs of light that dance around the treeline and, sometimes, dart about in the darkened rooms. A former resident reported that her cats had even played with the lights on occasion. These ghostly orbs were also sighted by would-be fisherman Brett Sipes, who had gone to the point in the early morning to cast off the county pier. It was still dark when Brett arrived, and as he unloaded his accoutrements he happened to glance up and spot a "ball of yellow fire" floating in the trees bordering the parking lot.

"I watched it for about five minutes," says Brett. "I'd never seen anything like it before in my life."

Brett looked on in amazement as several other orbs became visible farther back in the woods—orbs of blue, red, and yellow, bobbing and "twinkling" like Christmas lights in the black trees.

"I didn't feel unwelcome, exactly. I didn't have any kind of malicious feeling. But I knew I wasn't supposed to be there, and I didn't want to push it by taking a photo. So I left."

Madrona Point is certainly an imposing place. The trees here grow strangely in dense and sprawling groves, their branches twisting and tenting like the phalanges of a skeletal hand, and on winter days, when steel-grey waves pound the rocky shoreline and mist the air with spray, a wanderer standing at the tip of Madrona Point might well find his or herself finally in-tune with the "heart of the island"—and the weird legends that derive from the forested hills that curve around to enclose East Sound from either side.

Incidents at the Orcas Museum

"Haunted" houses can be found from Deer Harbor to Doe Bay—but in the heart of Eastsound, six original settler's cabins have been brought from across the island and merged into one structure: the Orcas Island Historical Museum. The Jackson, Kimple, Kirchhoff, Olsson, and John Boede, Jr. cabins were disassembled and then rebuilt around the John Boede, Sr. cabin in the 1950s, and numerous artifacts were subsequently donated, ranging from the island's first telephone switchboard to various pieces from the supposedly cursed collection of John Laurence Walsh (see the "Spirits from a Faraway Land" chapter of this book). It is a true melting pot of Orcas Island history, and as such lays claim to a multitude of bizarre stories.

One donation in particular may have contributed

to said activity. In 1924, a man named John Mattson —variously reported to be a resident of either Orcas or Shaw Island—uncovered a strange relic on his farm, a "bust" measuring sixteen inches in height and carved of a porous volcanic stone not found any-where in the vicinity.

"A front view of the idol, if we may call it such, is a very good likeness of the pictures of the great Egyptian sphinx. When placed face down and view-ed from the side it presents the exact form of a huge skull, minus the lower jaw bone," wrote the *Friday Harbor Journal*.

No one was sure of what the relic was or where it had come from, as it did not resemble any known native motifs; and it was surmised that, like other weird artifacts found elsewhere in the San Juans, it had been left by "one of the voyages made by Spanish, English and Bengal adventurers and traders during the last quarter of the 18th century." The "sphinx" eventually found its way to the Orcas mus-eum, although today its location is unknown.

Activity of a more ghostly nature has been reported at the museum over the years. Disembodied voices, phantom footsteps, and mysterious cold spots have all been encountered, along with the sounds of the old telephone switchboard being operated by some unseen force. Annette Rauch, a self-described "weekend historian," made mention of a few experiences of her own:

I was a part-time docent at the museum for about four

years, and there were a number of odd things that happened during my tenure. I would be working in the main office and I'd hear the sound of someone walking through the old cabins. These are old, creaky floorboards and the sound would reverberate if someone walked on them with heavy boots. On the occasions when this happened, the museum was closed to visitors and the doors were locked. I also saw one of our rocking chairs swaying of its own accord.

We had a visitor a few years ago who told us there were several ghosts in the museum. One, who she called "Mr. Johnny," was a man who had squatted in one of the cabins while it was abandoned during the Great Depression, and had drank himself to death. He was a malevolent sort who liked to scare visitors and move things around. Another was a Native American man who was connected to one of the artifacts in our indigenous room. And there was a Native woman, who our intern said was always bloodied and bruised, who may have been the wife of a settler. The woman who told us this called herself an "empath," which is someone who is apparently more sensitive to the spirit world than you or I.

Another visitor, Sharon Cosmidis of Tustin, California, mentioned having felt an oppressive atmosphere in one of the cabins.

"There was definitely a strong presence in one of the rooms. As soon as we walked in, it felt like we were intruding, like something didn't want us there, so I left, and the feeling just evaporated. That being said, I did feel like something was following us around the museum after that, but not necessarily in a dark kind of way. More like just keeping an eye on us.

"I'm not really sure why, but I mentioned what I'd felt to one of the docents on our way out, and as it turns out she wasn't surprised. She told me that a lot of visitors have had weird experiences, and a lot of them sound like mine. She mentioned too that she'd heard footsteps, heard voices, all this when the building was supposed to be empty, and even heard the place breathing at night. She said it was as a low, raspy inhale-exhale, and she could hear it in the oldest parts of the building. Really wild."

The Orcas Island Historical Museum, whether visited for the ghosts or for the more earthly exhibits, remains a premier island attraction, and deserves a prominent place on the discerning visitor's itinerary.

A Knock at the Door

Do the dead visit us? Can the specter of a man killed half a world away appear at the doorstep of those he loved? If a somewhat touching anecdote from the *Orcas Islander*'s February 5th, 1942 edition is to be believed, the answer would be a resounding yes.

The article reports the testimony of Mrs. Opal Whiteford Collins, of Deer Harbor, and her experience on a fall night in 1918. The author writes:

It was the night of September 29th, 1918, and as Mrs. Collins was stoking the fire—her husband, Mr. Charles Collins, being away on business—her thoughts drifted to her son, Charlie, Jr., and his whereabouts on that autumnal evening. Though letters from the front were censored much as they are today, the Collinses knew that their son was somewhere in northern France—although they had received no correspondence as of late. Mrs. Collins, naturally succumbing to the worrisome instinct of every mother whose son is away at war, continued stoking the fire, until there came a knock at the door—and to her shock, there stood none other than Charlie Jr.!

"Charlie!" exclaimed Mrs. Collins, but her words faltered as she took in the young man's haggard appearance. His doughboy uniform was tattered and caked with mud, and his helmet, an odd thing to wear home on furlough, was riddled with shrapnel. Charlie, whose eyes never made contact, said only: "I didn't make it across that field, ma. But we sure gave 'em hell." And with that, the figure of the young man faded away into the night air, and Mrs. Collins was left standing alone in the doorway, the import of this final knock at the door beginning to set in.

After a few weeks had passed, an official tele-gram arrived which bore the news of Charlie's death. The young private and his fellows had charged across an open field towards the Hun-held hamlet of Gesnes-en-Argonne, and somewhere in-between had fallen victim to the withering enfilade. Charlie's visit, it seemed, had come right at the moment of his demise.

[...] Of note is a final detail of Mrs. Collins's story: that spring, when the dormant bulbs of her flower garden began to blossom, a number of new-comers were apparent amongst the familiar crocuses and rhododendron: blood-red and orange poppies, as though transplanted from the fields of France, which can now be found scattered across the island—a melancholic reminder of the price our mothers and their sons pay for Old Glory and the nation it flutters above.

The *Orcas Islander*'s piece ran in the wake of Pearl Harbor and several other major Allied defeats, a time when many patriotic editorials were appearing in American newsprint. This story, though more than likely an Angel of Mons-esque attempt to boost morale, endures to the present day with its pathos and timely message.

The Little People

An odd phenomenon which appears and reappears across the pantheon of worldwide folklore is that of the "little people": elves, nymphs, gnomes, the Latin American *duende*, and other dwarf-like creatures who lurk in the trees and the dark corners of old homes, plotting mischief and occasionally stealing naughty children.

Orcas Island is naturally no exception to these far-reaching tales, and for countless generations stories have been passed down of these beings whom the Coast Salish knew as the *Kwak-wa-etai-mewh*, and whom the white settlers referred to as "gnomes" or, simply, "the Little People." They lived under root balls and beneath the enormous ant mounds on Mount Constitution, pelting interlopers with pebbles and, occasionally, tiny spears. These diminutive troublemakers were discussed at length by Mrs. Elva Hanway Deming in a 1944 *Orcas Islander* article:

When my husband's family first came up from Oregon, they proofed up a claim near the creek at Olga and I don't know what year it was but it was still a territory then. His father worked as a printer in Fairhaven in the winter and in the spring and summer he would return to the island to clear and plant. In the meantime, Alfred and his siblings were left alone at the homestead with their mother. It was during this time that my husband said many strange things took place.

The Indians who would camp sometimes at Stockade bay [an old name for Buck Bay] *to harvest clams and oysters paid a visit to the cabin one day and, in their rather coy way, gave a friendly warning to Mother Deming; that the gorge near their home, through which Bowman's creek* [Cascade Creek] *plunged to the sea, was the domain of the "little people"— strange little folk similar to our gnomes or elves, who are often the cause of trouble. The Indians warned that these gnomes were of a bad sort and were not to be trifled with. It was even suggested that offerings of food and trinkets be left on a certain rock at the gorge, although this was of course rejected by the family, who were Methodists.*

Over the years that my husband's family lived there, eggs, milk, produce from the root cellar, and an untold number of shiny metal objects vanished with-out a trace, which might ordinarily be blamed on raccoons or crows. But he and his brothers would often find odd and elaborate little contraptions made of woven grass and sticks left when an object would go missing, and so to them it must have been the gnomes from the gorge, even if no one ever saw them.

The old-timer Frank Worden* would also speak extensively of the Little People when he held court by the bonfire at North Beach—though his stories took on a considerably darker tone than Mrs. Deming's account. According to Worden, the Little People were malevolent beings, eager to attack passersby and lure children into the woods. He recounted the story of the Doe Bay schoolteacher, Mr. Whittell, who was riding alone into Eastsound many years ago when his horse reared up and refused to go further somewhere along the base of Mount Constitution. Whittell watched with terror as the monstrous anthills around him began to rupture and tiny creatures emerged, dark and mossy little men with turtleshell armor and miniature spears. Whittell, thinking quickly, reached into his saddlebag and began hurling apples at the pint-sized ambushers —Whittell's students left an assortment of apples on his desk every morning—and this seemed to distract the gnomes long enough to spur his mount and retreat. As it turned out, the Little People were known for their love of apples, and Whittell's reaction was enough to save his life.

Worden also told of how the Little People would mimic the sounds of children laughing or crying in the woods late at night, and how anyone foolish enough to follow the sounds would never be seen again. He told of a little boy who had wandered away from his parents' campsite, following the sounds, and had disappeared into the forest. The next morning, all that was found were a set of deep drag marks leading to a large anthill.

Though some would dismiss tales as simply remnants of the old European tradition of elves and gnomes, the historical significance of the *Kwak-wa-etai-mewh* to the Coast Salish should be enough to give one pause; could so many generations *really* be wrong? At the very least, when on a late-night stroll through the woods of Orcas Island, keep alert for the sounds of children playing in the dark—and what-ever you do, don't leave the trail . . .

Ghosts of Olga

Olga is one of those places where time slows to a crawl; the highway slopes down out of the dark timber of Moran park, following Cascade Creek, until the creek veers off toward Buck Bay and the road rolls on to the village. Mature poplar and maple shade the streets of quiet old homes, as does one weeping willow that descends, through multiple cuttings, from the tree that grew at Napoleon Bonaparte's grave on Saint Helena.

The setting hardly belies the hamlet's dark past; the Olga Tragedy of 1902 occurred here, of course, outside the old Moore place on the Doe Bay road; but that is only the most publicized incident. There were others, over the years, that are perhaps even more disturbing.

In 1915, a man named Clarence Sluyter seated himself on a case of blasting powder at Deer Point and blew himself up—as Orcas historian Fred John Splitstone wrote, "All that was ever found of his remains could have been put in a match box." Sluyter had reportedly been despondent over his poor health, and left a note for his wife reading, "I go to a watery grave. Never seek for me, because I can't be found."

As the son-in-law of early settler John Viereck, was interred at the Viereck Cemetery in Doe Bay.

Later, Deer Point would become the site of a sprawling and secluded estate that hosted lavish Hollywood parties into the 1970s. These low-profile events would often carry over to remote Spieden Island, where guests, including prominent politicians, would hunt mouflon sheep and other exotic animals. It is unknown if any ghostly activity has ever been reported at the Deer Point estate in connection with either of these blow-outs.

A similarly tragic incident took place at the Olga Store—the owner, Duncan Bower, committed suicide there in 1934. As a result, the Olga Store is said to be haunted . . . though it should be mentioned that the current store was built in 1937, and the original, where Bower shot himself, was closer to the waterfront.

"The air always felt heavy going in there by yourself," says Chuck Nash*, a forty-year Olga resident. "When it was open, it was a nice, breezy kind of place. But later on, after it had been closed for a few years, it got a lot spookier."

Indeed, the Olga Store has sat empty for well over

a decade, its white paint peeling and the old 76 gas-pumps rusting away in the salt air. Chuck recalled an incident experienced by a neighbor during this time, well over a decade ago:

"My neighbor did a little work over there, touching up the siding and replacing some deck boards. [The owner] had given him the keys so he could go in and check for leaks [...] one night we had a big rainstorm come through, and he decided to walk over and check."

Chuck's neighbor, shining his flashlight into the dark store, saw a shadowy figure crouched in the corner. The neighbor quickly realized that his flashlight beam, though pointed directly at the shadow, was having no effect . . . the shadow was still a featureless black void that almost seemed to "absorb" the light. The neighbor fled the scene and only returned in the morning to shut the door—and then never returned again.

"We all like to tell stories, don't we?" muses Chuck.

Despite all these dark deeds of the distant past, not all is downcast and macabre in Olga. A more uplifting tale of the supernatural takes place at Gray's Beach, the low-bank strand just west of Olga Park. The land had once belonged to John W. Gray, a Kentuckian who had drifted north from the California goldfields and eventually found his way to the Queen Charlotte Islands of British Columbia. While camping on one of the islands, Gray happened to spot an Indian canoe that was adrift and seemingly abandoned, and so he paddled out for a closer look —and was shocked to find a beautiful young Haida girl lying inside, bleeding out from a slashed throat. Gray was quick to administer aid, and when the girl had recovered enough to speak she told a shocking tale: namely, that her entire tribe had died of smallpox, and that she had paddled out to sea and cut her own throat so that she might rejoin her family in the afterlife.

Gray married the girl, Ketonah, and settled in Olga in the early 1870s. They raised a family of six, and were later joined for a period by John L. Morrison, a well-known Oregon pioneer and namesake of the Portland street and bridge. The Grays lived comfortably at Olga, and for many years their idyllic homestead was the site of an awe-inspiring spectacle—every other spring, a pair of massive, elaborately-carved canoes could be seen gliding out of the early-morning fog and landing at Gray's Beach—a sight that, in earlier days, would have heralded a howling and blood-mad frenzy. These visitations to the Gray place were hardly warlike, however—for Mrs. Gray, as it happened, was the daughter of a high chief, and the Haida would come to bring gifts and to visit with their far-flung princess—who could never speak above a whisper.

According to local legend, these annual visits never ended with Mrs. Gray's passing in 1894. Some say the canoes still land at the old Gray place on foggy evenings, and that ghostly cookfires can be seen flickering on the beach when the stars are just right—though others claim that the fires were more likely from the smugglers who once anchored their sloops there.

The old Olga Cemetery seemingly produced a tale of the shambling undead. In 1922, a Doe Bay resident submitted the following odd encounter to the *Friday Harbor Journal* under the initials "R.G.":

I was passing an Orcas Island cemetery late one evening, returning home, when suddenly a tombstone tumbled over and the head of a man and finally the whole body of a man arose from under it. The man was ragged and unkempt. He seemed very thin and looked very strange. He walked rather unsteadily to the fence and climbed over, and then went down the road in the direction of Olga. With wildly beating heart I watched the apparition until it disappeared—for that was what I deemed it to be.

Being of a scientific mind I determined to examine the grave. Could it be possible that there are really such things as spooks? I went to the grave, to which the headstone had been replaced by the spook before leaving. I examined it closely, but could find nothing of scientific value, either as proof or disproof of the theory of spooks. I felt very nervous and unsteady and could not walk as steadily as usual. Accidentally I bumped against the tombstone, which gave way. I fell down into a deep hole under it.

I immediately jumped to my feet when I reached the bottom, feeling very much excited. Had the spook returned and thrown me into the grave for my inquisitiveness? This was the conclusion I had reached. In my excitement I had began pacing up and down. There seemed to be an extensive shaft or room under that graveyard. I imagined that I must now be dead, and perhaps I too should be haunting those that are still alive.

Suddenly I heard distant singing. I thought perhaps this must be the dead people having a good time. Since I was now a dead man too, I determined to go and join them and have a good time myself. There is no use crying over spilt milk, you know.

So I went toward the sound. Suddenly I bumped into a door, which I opened to find myself in a lighted room, full of many people. The room itself was fitted out like a saloon of the old days. I stepped up to the bar and asked for a glass of buttermilk, for I never drank anything stronger. The bartender looked at me keenly, and said they had no such thing.

The place is nothing more nor less than a concealed blind pig [speakeasy]. *The tombstone covers and hides the entrance, and is hinged on. There is a ladder from the top to the bottom of the shaft. The bottom shaft runs far back under the mountain to the barroom.*

I talked with several persons present. There were men from all over the county, from many parts of the state, and even from Oregon, California and other places. That grave will add to the popularity of the Islands during the coming summer, no doubt. After a while I went out and returned home.

Whether or not the ghosts of Olga are still serving spirits remains, naturally, to be seen . . .

Odd Happenings at the Odd Fellows Hall

Though relatively unassuming now, the old meeting hall that sits nestled along the rocky shore of Madrona Point was once at the very center of social life on Orcas Island. The Independent Order of Odd Fellows emerged on Orcas at the height of the so-called "Golden Age of Fraternalism" in America, a time when the Odd Fellows outnumbered even the Masons, and in 1891 the Mount Constitution Lodge No. 88 was established in Eastsound.

Its original membership was considerably different from today's long-haired and tie-dyed cadre—the Odd Fellows of old were known for their Masonic regalia and secretive ceremonies involving human skeletons and esoteric symbolism. However, their spirit of community outreach and general mirth has remained constant throughout the years, and today the hall hosts dances and other events much as it always has. It is only natural, then, that an admittedly "odd" place should play host to a litany of paranormal phenomena as well.

The original lodge burned to the ground on the night of January 2nd, 1950, allegedly because a member had tried to thaw-out the frozen plumbing with a blowtorch after a severe nor'easter. The building was a total loss; the night was so cold that the water had frozen in the firehoses. Nevertheless, volunteers rallied to erect the present-day replacement soon after. The new hall boasted a restaurant kitchen and a slick new dancefloor, in addition to the basement ceremonial chambers not often opened to the public.

Mike Hartinger, an active I.O.O.F. booster, was a volunteer custodian at the hall for many years, and had this to say on the subject of strange happenings:

"Sure, there's some weird things that happen around there. I remember one time, I was cleaning up the kitchen after everyone had left, and I started hearing what sounded like a big gathering upstairs, like a dance maybe. I turned down the radio and sure enough, you could hear people talking, murmuring, footsteps, all that. But turned down a few decibels, if that makes sense. And there was 50s-type music playing. I went upstairs to see what the heck was going on, and everything stopped as soon as I walked in. The floor was totally empty. That happened a few times, actually, and the third time I just ignored it.

"Sometimes I'd have my dog with me, and she'd start acting real weird sometimes. There was this one room she'd always refuse to go into, even when I was in there sweeping or whatever. She'd start growling and her hair would stand up, and she'd just be staring off into the corner of the room like there was something there looking back at us. That's the room where we kept the skeleton. I called him 'Bonesy'. Anyway, I didn't like that room too much."

True to their name, the Odd Fellows were well-known for using human skeletons in their elaborate initiation rites. The original Mount Constitution Lodge was said to have utilized an eight-foot tall, "Neanderthal"-like cadaver uncovered near Buck Mountain in the early 1900s, at least according to Orcas old-timer Bill McWilliams*—a man with an admitted proclivity for tall tales. The current lodge's skeleton, last seen publicly in the 1980s, has a similarly enigmatic origin; lodge member Pat Gore said that the skeleton had been ordered from a medical supply company sometime after the 1950 fire, while Ron Metcalf maintained that it was unearthed from a midden on Madrona Point. Whatever the case may be, the presence of mysterious remains at the old hall can hardly hurt the chances of paranormal happenings.

Mark Vuorma, a restaurateur who helped operate a "pop-up" establishment in the Odd Fellows base-ment, also made mention of a multitude of spine-tingling encounters in the old building.

"I would be working there three or four days a week in the summer, and I'd usually be the one closing up [...] there's some weird stuff that happens around there, for sure. I used to hear music coming from the dancefloor, like old time stuff, which was pretty eerie, and you'd hear voices. You'd hear footsteps when it was empty. We'd open up in the morning and the faucets would be running, which wasn't great because of the water bills [...] I would say one of the weirdest things was when the temperature would drop out of nowhere, almost to where you could see your breath. Like standing in a walk-in fridge. It felt like something was in the room with you.

"There was an old player piano in the other room, and I heard it play on its own sometimes. Which doesn't sound crazy, I know, because it's a player piano, but you have to pump it to make it work, and I was the only one home, you know?

"My friend Erica said she was putting up some decorations in the main hall, by herself, and there's this big floor-to-ceiling black curtain on the far wall. Like a stage curtain. She said she looked over and there was someone moving around behind the curtain. She called out, you know, 'who's there?', and it stopped moving. Didn't say anything back. It just stood there behind the curtain, and, you know, that was pretty unsettling, so she left. We don't know if that was a person trespassing or what, but that's really not normal behavior, right? And, again, there shouldn't have been anyone in there besides her."

A former Noble Grand of the Mount Constitution Lodge, Bob Daynes*, wrote the following in correspondence with the author:

The Odd Fellows Lodge is an inherently spiritual place, given that an I.O.O.F. Lodge is also a temple, both to the universal wisdom and to the Supreme Being. I think you'll find that most Lodges hold a spiritual power, although it's really no different than the mystique one would find in a cathedral or synagogue. Of course there is spirituality in these places; a temple, no matter the religion, is a place decorated with esoterica and symbology that holds tremendous power; whether this power is confined to the mind, I suppose, is up for debate.

What, if anything, lurks in the shadows of the old Odd Fellows hall? Is it the residuals of past dances and ceremonies? The spirit of the skeleton "Bonesy" wandering the empty rooms? Or could it be something even stranger? As always, there is only one sure way to find out . . .

Out of the Depths

The riptide was long known for the strange creatures that it dredged up from the deep channels surrounding Orcas Island—eyeless things with spindly limbs and gaping maws—and islanders would often report sightings of the legendary sea serpent "Caddy," or *Cadborosaurus*, as it undulated through the dark waterways. . . though on Orcas, this cryptic creature was first known by another name entirely: "Ugly Elsie."

The story of Ugly Elsie began in May of 1909, when, according to a 1962 *Orcas Islander* piece by Carrell J. Colmery, Jim Baker and his crew were corralling logs off the north shore.

Three boatmen in two boats were busy collecting piling logs that were drifting away toward the rip tide that had started to run off Terrill's Beach on the north shore of Orcas Island. It was a sunny day in May, 1909.

The loggers had attached tow lines to several of the logs and were bringing them back to the log raft they were forming at the terminus of the skid road and in the salt chuck at the base of a cliff.

Jim was ashore with a team of horses. His view took in the three men in the boat, the reef off shore which was crawling with a herd of seals and beyond in the deep water a school of spouting blackfish.

Suddenly the seals hastily left the reef and the blackfish, evidently alarmed, changed course and headed toward the boatmen. Jim shouted a warning to them. Then his eye caught a boiling in the waters beyond the reef, and there arose a great leviathan of the deep, a sea serpent.

As the creature surfaced Jim could see about 30 feet of its body. Its head, which was raised five feet in the air was about the size of that of a large draft horse. Its dorsal fin back from the head about 15 feet stood in the air at a height of approx.- imately six feet. The fin was flexible and moved to right and left like the trunk of an elephant. The fore part of the creature came out of the water onto the reef. Attached to its head and neck there was a mane of feelers.

As the sea monster slid off the reef it twisted its head and evidently spotted the three men in the dories, for it started in their direction. Jim Baker shouted to them of its approach and the men glancing in its direction abandoned their tow lines and with oars and paddles rowed for their lives toward the shore.

The sea serpent swam to the abandoned logs and after nudging them turned away and headed in the direction of Sucia

Island leaving a foamy wake that was long visible.

"Curley Bob, one of the dorymen, shouted to me, 'It's Ugly Elsie'," wrote Jim.

The fact that Curley Bob gave the creature a name indicates that it was a familiar sight to Islanders. And such indeed was the case, for hundreds of people had long range views of the creature over a period of ten years.

The more common taxonym of *Cadborosaurus* was assigned by a Victoria journalist named Archie Wills in 1933, to describe an identical creature that had been sighted in Haro Strait by several well-respected men. A rash of "Caddy" encounters dominated the early 1930s, including several reports from American waters—fishermen in Port Angeles had taken to calling the creature "Old Hiaschuckoluk," meaning "old camel-face" in the native dialect—although it is unknown why the local Indians would have a word for "camel." Another name for the creature was, more bluntly, "Bosco."

In 1995, a serious scientific study was published by Dr. Paul LeBlond and Dr. Edward Bousfield, both prominent marine biologists and Fellows of the Royal Society of Canada, which catalogs numerous accounts dating back to the 19th century and earlier. LeBlond and Bousfield posit that there is a long and skinny creature, falling into the class *reptilia*, living in the cold and murky waters of the inland sea. The researchers even cited ancient petroglyphs found along the Nanaimo River depicting a dragon-like creature, and stories of the *hiyitl'iik*, a sea serpent from Manhousat tribal lore. A supernatural serpent called *sisiutl* is also found in the mythology of several northwestern tribes.

Jim Baker's would not be the only sighting reported on Orcas. Another *Orcas Islander* article, this time dating from August of 1941, mentions a mass sighting in Harney Channel by passengers aboard the steamer *Waialeale* in 1912, and quotes an unnamed newspaper from the period:

[...] *According to Mr. W.H. Leffingwell, of the Seattle Cement Laundry Tray Co., he and several other sightseers were gathered on the promenade at around 11 o'clock when a monstrous serpent was sighted in the channel about 300yds. off. The serpent was described as around 60ft. long and covered in brownish scales, with a coarse mane of hair about its neck resembling that of a horse. Mr. Leffingwell noted that it swam in a curious burrowing motion, rising and falling above the waves in the fashion of a caterpillar. The spectators observed the creature for around half an hour as it sported in the waters near Broken Point, causing the sea to roil and foam considerably, before it dove out of sight and was seen no more.*

Mr. Leffingwell says that the pilot is all-too familiar with these creatures and was unperturbed by its gamboling, having told the excited onlookers of his run-in with a similar serpent in Birch Bay some years ago, and of the serpents that are regularly encountered in the waters near San Diego, Cal., and the Coronado Islands. Mr. Leffingwell and others hope that such a large-scale sighting will spur a scientific study of this hitherto unknown species and its associated genera.

The veracity of this account, naturally, is unknown.

Another apparent "Caddy" sighting took place thirty years later, though it was never published in a newspaper. In 1942, following the attack on Pearl Harbor, widespread fears of a Japanese invasion led to the formation of the Orcas Island Air Observers, a civil defense group with observation posts at key points around the island. In the spring of that year, Elwyn Goddard was manning the eight p.m. to midnight shift at the Deer Harbor post when he spotted something massive undulating through the moonlit water. According to Goddard's grandson, Brian, it was a "thirty-foot sea serpent" with a head like "a cross between a horse and a leopard seal." Goddard was deeply unnerved and fired on the creature with his rifle, missing it twice, before it dove down and vanished into the black.

"He told my dad that story when he was a kid, after he'd had a few drinks," says Brian. "I will say, he never liked going out on the water."

Keoni Davis*, who ran a whale-watching vessel out of Deer Harbor for many years, had at least one run-in to report. In 2006, while taking a handful of tourists out towards Stuart Island, Davis spotted what he initially took to be a log floating between Orcas and Spieden Island. His assumption was shattered when the "log" reared up ten feet into the air and spouted water like a breaching whale. The creature, clearly serpentine, was glossy black like a sea lion, and Davis estimated that it must have been about forty feet long and as girthy as a fifty-five-gallon drum. The serpent appeared to observe the whale-watchers before continuing on its way, swimming in its familiar "up and down" motion, eventually disappearing from sight near Waldron Island.

"I've never seen anything like it before or since," said Davis. "The worst part of it was, we had a lady who wouldn't stop screaming for us to get out of there [...] even though it was headed in the opposite direction. Most of us were just trying to get a look at it!"

Davis says that footage from the incident likely exists, as at least one witness had been filming with a camcorder . . . although, perhaps unsurprisingly, nothing of the kind has ever surfaced.

* * *

Serpents were not the only sea creatures encountered on Orcas in the old days. George Gale, a well-known painter who lived near the ferry landing, had a terrifying run-in with a monstrously-large "devilfish," or octopus, in the summer of 1930. He had first observed the massive mollusk four years earlier, when it had moved into a low, tide-level cave near Gale's home and begun consuming the surrounding sea-life at an alarming rate. The creature's size and strategic hideout had allowed it to ravage Gale's clambeds and fishing grounds unmolested until the June of 1930, when the moon was at apogee and the tide had ebbed far out into Harney Channel, leaving the cave fully exposed. Gale grabbed an axe and a crowbar and climbed down to the cave, and was shocked at what he found; a mountainous midden of clamshells blocked the entrance, backed by a neat wall of flat and carefully selected stones, which served to block the clams from collapsing into the cave, and to keep a sufficient amount of saltwater inside to sustain the devilfish through the low tides. Gale, though impressed, set to work demolishing the bulwark, and quickly met resistance from the lurker in the cave.

The devilfish lashed out with its long tentacles, longer and girthier than any ever seen in those waters before, or perhaps anywhere, for that matter . . . the creature, far back within the cave, seized Gale's crowbar—but before it could get a better hold and draw him in, Gale managed to strike a series of fatal blows with the axe and vanquish the devilfish before it could do likewise.

The creature, when laid out on the nearby beach, proved to be much larger than even had Gale had thought as he had fought the thing—and it must have seemed quite monstrous then. Old-timers compared it to the colossal specimens that Indians had hauled into Anacortes in the 1880s, things so large they had made newsprint across the northwest . . . though Gale's devilfish dwarfed even those.

Regardless of how true any of these tales may be, at least two takeaways remain clear: to keep your eyes peeled when you're on the water or exploring sea caves, and to row like the wind for shore when "Caddy" is on the hunt for killer whales . . .

How Victim Island Got Its Name

For many years, visitors to West Sound have found the area's impressive beauty at odds with the stark and grisly names that appear on local charts—Mass-acre Bay, Skull Island, and Victim Island; names that, to the old-timers, conjure tales of bloodsoaked nights in the distant past, and to the uninitiated, tingle the spine with their strangely violent evocations.

These names derive from a particularly terrible incident in 1858. A large band of Lummi had been encamped at the head of West Sound, by the bay that nestles below the southern spur of Ship Peak. One night a warfleet of Stikine—or in some accounts, Haida—raiders landed on the beach and set upon the sleeping village. Warclubs slashed in the dark and musketfire cracked and echoed across the waters as an early white settler, remembered now only as "Old Deshau," looked on in horror from the hill. As the raiders departed, Old Deshau crept down from his hiding place and observed over one hundred dead on the beach. This incident would inspire the terrifying toponymy found on later maps.

Victim Island, located just south of Massacre Bay, is a three-acre islet no different from any other. It rises to a prominence of forty-five feet and sits just over three hundred and fifty feet off the rocky coast of Camp Four Winds. Its high walls rise up like a battle-scarred fortress, fractured and scoured deeply by the receding glaciers, and offer a formidable challenge to the Four Winds campers and other visitors. The forest above is a rarity in the Pacific Northwest—Garry oak grows together with madrona and fir and wizened juniper out of the glacial till and cracks in the bedrock, a remnant of a forest-type that was once common prior to white settlement. And that is when the name "Victim" supposedly came about; according to a story passed down from early settlers, Victim Island is where an Indian princess met her untimely fate.

A 1942 *Orcas Islander* article laid the story bare— the author had apparently found the tale in a filebox from the collection of Ethan Allen, a Waldron Island homesteader who had been the county school superintendent and a noted conservator of Indian artifacts. As the article relates:

In the very old days there had been an Indian princess who was deathly afraid of the water, but whose band lived on the westerly shore of West Sound. One day while she was out walking, the princess met a young brave from another band on the other side of the sound at White Beach bay, and the two quickly fell in love, although the parents of these two lovers hardly approved, as the bands were rivals. The princess's father posted guards to keep the girl from leaving the village through the forest, so confident was he that she wouldn't dare to cross the sound. She did yet manage, however, to get a message to the young man, telling him to meet her on what today is Victim island.

So the princess snuck away in the night and took a canoe. She had never been on the water before, but she managed to overcome her fear so long she was on a boat. She paddled to the island and waited for her paramour. But the young man had been found out, and he had been restrained from going. She waited all night long, and finally decided that she'd been jilted and went to leave, heartbroken . . . but she discovered that her canoe had drifted away in the dark, and now her only choice was to swim ashore, which was only a few hundred feet away . . . but the princess was so terrified by the water that she simply couldn't. She called out for help, hoping that someone would come to save her, but no one came. The tyees of both bands had met and decided that it would be in the interest of peace to let the girl stay where she was . . . for the lovers had upset the balance of power, and she had made her own prison. The young man, meanwhile, was put to death for his disobedience.

The princess could be seen day after day screaming for help, pleading with passing fishermen to rescue her . . . they could

207

hear her cries from either end of the sound. But no one saved her. Eventually she withered away and was heard from no more. And so the story goes that, to this very day, you can still hear the cries of the princess echoing over the water on certain evenings, begging in vain for rescue, and the brave will appear out of the fog in his canoe, still searching for his lost love...

While this tale is almost certainly a "romance" in the style of popular literature of the time, the ghostly remnants of the slaughters that took place at West Sound continue to haunt the green waters and the high forests that slope up to looming Turtleback. In the early 20th century, a road crew unearthed several skeletons there while straightening a curve, and over the years many more were found bleached white and scattered over Skull Island, at the head of Massacre Bay. West Sound, and little Victim Island, will be forever haunted—if not by wandering specters, then by the gruesome names that remind us of a time when life was not so peaceful on Orcas Island.

Lost Treasures

There is hardly anything so alluring to a young person's imagination as the prospect of buried treasure—the thought of gold coins spilling from long-rotted chests buried in the lonely hills is enough to excite even the most seasoned of treasure seekers. Frank Worden* often told of the various lost fortunes that are supposedly cached across the island, expounding gleefully as the children's eyes widened and thoughts of pirate's loot and shiny new toys filled their heads . . .

One of these fortunes is said to be in a hidden cave. An old tale states that an unnamed British tar had jumped ship in Victoria during the Pig War days and lit out for the islands, where he purchased a "klootchman"—or Indian wife—and stashed his loot in a small limestone cave while he avoided the authorities. The British didn't want the tar simply because he'd deserted, however—he had also absconded with a chest of gold sovereigns from the ship's paymaster, and the captain's silver tea set, which had once belonged to Lord Nelson himself. The tar, fatefully, would never be able to enjoy his ill-gotten riches—he was later found dead in his hideout, scalped and mutilated, with his wife nowhere to be found. It was speculated that she had told her brothers of the loot, and that they had tortured the man to determine its location . . . but none of the sovereigns ever resurfaced, nor did the tea set, meaning the tar likely took his secret to the grave.

Orcas is said to be honeycombed with such caves —scoured out of the porous limestone by the waves of ancient and since-receded seas. Several are known and recorded, while others are only whispered of, such as the fabled caverns beneath Mount Constitution. Fowler's Cave, hidden above a pasture near the likewise-named pond, extends back some fifteen feet, and was long used as shelter by the resident sheep. Orkila Cave, located on the first small point southeast of Point Doughty, was a rumored refuge for smugglers in the early days—with entrances on the beach and far above on the cliffs, it would have made a fine and strategic redoubt. Similar caves are found near West Beach and Lookout Mountain, and a particularly extensive system yawns wide at the old Imperial Lime Quarry northwest of Massacre Bay. Other caves, unfortunately, such as those on Flaherty's Hill and near Dolphin Bay, were destroyed by quarrying in earlier days—and no riches were reported found.

Another treasure tale, favored by Frank Worden, concerns the lost "Bleeding Heart Mine" on Mount Constitution. As the story goes, three men went out prospecting during the "gold rush" days of the 1890s and eventually found a mineralized outcropping near Bleeding Heart Springs—now known as Cold Springs. They sunk a prospect hole and quickly realized that they had struck a vein of silver to rival the old Virginia City mines. The trio soon fell to arguing, however, as each man felt that he deserved a larger share than the rest, and soon pistols were drawn. When the smoke cleared, only one man remained standing. Realizing his predicament, he dragged the bodies into the hole and backfilled the entrance before making his escape, never to return.

Some years later, a local man decided to try and relocate the diggings, despite others warning him that the site was haunted. After only a day or two of searching he showed up at the Olga store, proudly proclaiming that he had found the lost Bleeding Heart Mine, and that he would begin excavating in the morning. The old-timers could only shake their heads. When he failed to return by week's end, searchers climbed up to the old claim and found the hole freshly filled in, and the man's foot sticking out of the rubble. Upon pulling him out, they noted his face—it was twisted in terror, and on his throat were the marks of a skeletal hand . . .

The old-timers also spoke of the mysterious "stone anchor" on the summit of Turtleback Mountain. Apparently, at some unknown date in the distant past, a sailing ship had grounded on the northern end of the island and the sailors had trekked up Turtleback to lay out the shape of an anchor in stone, an arm of which allegedly points to a buried treasure. The outline of an anchor does indeed exist on Turtleback, stretching out nearly thirty-five feet on a mossy bald at the summit, and no one knows just who made it; experts have pointed out that the style of the anchor is pre-1820.

"The hook and crossbar of the anchor measured ten feet wide and the distance between them is fifteen feet," wrote W.R. Giffin in a 1940 *Orcas Islander* piece. "There is a row of rocks extending out from the anchor for a distance of twenty feet, representing the chain. The rocks are all carefully placed, indicating that great pains were taken in producing this representation of an anchor."

Giffin further noted that the anchor had been ancient even when the first settlers had arrived in the early 1850s:

I have been told knowledge on the existence of this anchor dates back for 80 years, at the time William Miller came to the Island in 1852. When Omer Freel was a small lad, Mr. Miller told him he saw it soon after he arrived on the island, and at that time it was covered in moss. Being interested in this curiosity, Mr. Miller said he talked to many of the older Indians about it, and was generally told that in years gone by there had been a ship wrecked on the northern side of the Island, and that the survivors of the wreck climbed to the top of the mountain to get their bearings and while there made the anchor.

Mr. Freel says that when he first saw the anchor 35 years ago it was still covered with moss, but ten years later a fire burned over the summit of the mountain, and burned the moss off the rocks. At present there is still some moss growing on the bottom edges of the rocks, but the tops are still bare and smooth. If the rocks were covered with moss 80 years ago, it would indicate the anchor had been made many years prior to that time, as but little moss has accumulated during the past 25 years, or since the fire.

Theories as to the anchor's origins abounded. Ethan Allen, "the Sage of the San Juans," proposed that the stones had been laid as a survey marker by Spanish explorers in 1791.

"The anchor would be a monument that would prove their having been here," wrote Allen. "I have no doubt but that they carried their instruments up there and ascertained its longitude and latitude. All of which, including its dimensions, position, etc., were carefully set down in the captain's journal and are now in the archives of Mexico or Spain."

Some said, alternately, that the wreck was a Spanish treasure galleon—thrown far off-course from its regular route between Acapulco and Manila—while others contended that it was a Japanese trader caught in the *Kuroshio* current.

"A Seattle man who has spent a fortune researching the subject said Spanish ships visited points along the Pacific Coast in bygone days, caching treasure for future use in colonizing the area," said local historian David Richardson. "The locations were always marked by cryptic arrangements of stones."

Richardson also discussed the theories of Frank Mullis, a well-known scholar of San Juan history.

"[Mullis] told us of an ancient sailing ship that was recovered in the nearby Wasp Island area and surmised survivors of an early wreck lived out their lives as castaways here long years ago."

In truth, the rock arrangements on Turtleback, which also include a cairn and a compass rose, were likely the work of Charles Wilkes's survey expedition in the early 1840s—a nearby boulder inscribed "HULL," the name they had assigned to Orcas, seems to bear out this belief. Nevertheless, there was a common theory amongst the New Agers that the compass and the anchor were a part of a series of strange, mystic symbols found on other island promontories such as Blakely Peak and Mount Dallas. Interestingly, a second stone compass can indeed be found near Cold Springs on Mount Constitution.

Treasure-hunters are known to have combed the mountain in years past, and one man was said to have rushed into town excitedly raving of a secret tunnel he'd found in the mountainside. The old-timers, exchanging grins, informed the man that the tunnel was an old prospect dug by Ed Warbass in the 1880s.

An intriguing item from the *San Juan Islander* of November 26th, 1903 does lend significant credence to the treasure tales, however. The article, titled "Did Pinneo Have a Pipe Dream?", reads:

A strange tale comes from Deer Harbor that reminds one of the hair-raising stories of Capt. Kidd and the buccaneers of the Spanish main. It is told by Fred Pinneo, who was made to play a part in it that made him extremely uncomfortable for a day or two.

He says that while he was at work cutting cordwood for the Deer Harbor Lime Company on its property and only about a quarter of a mile from its kiln Thursday afternoon about four o'clock four strange men suddenly appeared before him in the woods—all dark, swarthy foreigners, who talked among themselves in a language unknown to him. One of them is described as a man of immense size, fully six feet and a half in height, armed with two big revolvers and a long knife. Another was a very old man, apparently upwards of ninety, whose tottering steps two of the younger men supported.

This venerable old chap directed the others to a large rock, overgrown with moss and which had evidently been undisturbed for many years. This big boulder was turned over and from underneath it a black bottle was taken and on the spot where the bottle lay a compass was set and certain bearings taken. The stump of a tree which Mr. Pinneo had felled was measured and the measurements taken for identification with data which the party had. Pinneo was then ordered not to follow them or report their presence to anyone until some of the party returned and gave him permission to do so, and the promises required were given with alacrity. The mysterious party then departed and disappeared into the shadows of the forest and Pinneo remained in his cabin alone all night awaiting their return with wonder not unmixed with fear.

About the middle of the following day they returned, made some more observations and again left, telling Pinneo that he was free to depart in peace, which he lost no time in doing. He says that soon after the party left he saw a boat pull out toward the north with four men in it. None of their talk among themselves was intelligible to him, only one—he of the giant stature, revolvers and bowie knife, seeming to have any knowledge of English. Mr. Pinneo told his experience to Foreman Paxson, of the Island Lime Company, as soon as he could find him and the latter does not question the truth of the story, much as it seems like a "pipe dream" or carefully concocted hoax.

It is said that somewhere in that vicinity there are a lot of boulders arranged in the form of an anchor and which have long been known to a few "old settlers" as the "rock anchor." The overturned and moss-grown boulder may have been one of these.

Some contend, also, that the treasure is not located on Orcas at all—rather, it is buried on neighboring Flattop Island, where an arm of the anchor points.

The remote coastline around Point Doughty and the Glenwood Inn, allegedly a "robber's roost" for smugglers, rumrunners, and other dangerous characters in the late 19th century, is said to conceal a fortune in precious gems. One of these desperadoes was Henry Wagner, better known as the "Flying Dutchman," a vicious man who had once been a member of Butch Cassidy's "Hole-in-the-Wall" gang. Supposedly the Dutchman had brought in a sizable number of stolen jewels, which he had then cached somewhere along the northwestern shore. Misfortune befell the outlaw, however—he was arrested and hanged for shooting a policeman on Vancouver Island—and so the jewels remain hidden, awaiting some lucky and well-attuned wanderer.

Today, the lost treasures of Orcas Island remain lost; but is that really such a bad thing? A simple walk through the woods becomes a treasure hunt, and youngsters, giddy with thoughts of buried gold, roam the beaches with trowels and create memories that last a lifetime—and old men with metal detectors smile, not knowing what the next sweep may bring.

Afterword

Are there answers to be had? Strange tales of shipwrecks, lost mines, and ghostly figures wandering the lonely backroads and beaches are bound to elicit more than a few questions in the average reader. Is Orcas really a "power spot" or "window area," a kind of stop-over on the interdimensional highway? Does limestone conduct psychic energy? Does Raven still perch atop Mount Constitution? As a historian, that's hardly my area of expertise, and as a journalist, I adhere to the old adage, "A man who is all theory is like a rudderless ship on a shoreless sea." Speculation is reserved for you, the reader. I am only the messenger.

The very nature of a book of this sort is one of hearsay, rumor, and, above all, the power of suggestion. In my search for these stories, I sought out many old-time islanders whose memories and hidden-away steamer trunks of musty letters and motheaten scrapbooks proved invaluable, and whose extensive interviews led me down a myriad of so-called "rabbit holes." Sadly, length is always a consideration with this type of publication, as is the effect that bringing many of these stories to light may bring, and so this book is shorter than it perhaps could have been. Nevertheless, I believe that the stories here are the real "meat and potatoes," so to speak, and would be of the most interest to students of Orcas Island folklore.

And so, reader, if you should find yourself roaming the island byways on a moonlit night, when owls hoot and the trees writhe in the icy breeze, rem-ember what you've learned here, and even if you're snug in a cozy and lamplit room with the wind crashing harmlessly against the panes, know that even then, that creaking in the bowels of the house may be something else entirely . . . something far more ghastly than anything you've *speculated* it may be.

Bibliography

BOOKS

- Bagley, Clarence B. *Indian Myths of the Northwest.* Seattle: Lowman and Hanford, 1930

- Bailey-Cummings, Jo and Al Cummings. *San Juan: the Powder-Keg Island.* Friday Harbor: Beach Combers, 1987

- Bailey, Jo and Carl Nyberg. *Gunkholing in the San Juans.* Seattle: Nor'westing Publishing, 1985

- Bancroft, Hubert Howe. *The History of Washington, Idaho, and Montana.* San Francisco: The History Company, 1890

- Blanchard, Norman C. and Stephen Wilen. *Knee-Deep in Shavings: Memories of Early Yachting and Boatbuilding on the West Coast.* Victoria: Touch-Wood Editions, 1999

- Burn, June. *100 Days in the San Juans: A 1946 Voyage Through the San Juan Islands.* Friday Harbor: Long House Printcrafters & Publishers, 1983

- Burn, June. *Living High: An Unconventional Autobiography*. Friday Harbor: Griffin Bay Bookstore, 1992

- Bushman, Donald Otto. *The Geography of Orcas Island*. Seattle: University of Washington Press, 1949

- Calkins, R.H. *High Tide*. Seattle: Marine Digest Publishing Company, 1952

- Carlson, Glenn and Mildred Carlson. *The Rosario Story*. Everett, Washington: Alexander Printing Company, 1967

- Clark, Ella E. *Indian Legends of the Pacific Northwest*. Berkeley: University of California Press, 1953

- Crawford, Jack. *Time Shadows & Tall Tales: San Juan Island in Earlier Years*. Friday Harbor: Illumina, 2010

- Curtis, Edward S. *The North American Indian: Being a Series of Volumes Picturing and Describing the Indians of the United States, The Dominion of Canada, and Alaska, Volume 9*. New York: E.S. Curtis, 1913

- Danner, Wilbert R. *Limestone Resources of Western Washington*. Olympia: Washington Department of Conservation, 1966

- Downs, Art. *Outlaws & Lawmen of Western Canada: Volume 2*. Victoria: Heritage House Publishing, 2006

- Edson, Lelah Jackson. *The Fourth Corner: Highlights from the Early Northwest*. Bellingham, Washington: Cox Brothers, Inc., 1951

- Faber, Jim. *Steamer's Wake*. Seattle: Enetai Press, 1985

- Gibbs, Jim and Joe Williamson. *Maritime Memories of Puget Sound*. West Chester, Pennsylvania: Schiffer Publishing, 1987

- Halliday, William R. *Caves of Washington*. Olympia: Washington Department of Conservation, 1963

- Hauck, Dennis William. *Haunted Places, the National Directory: Ghostly Abodes, Sacred Sites, UFO Landings, and Other Supernatural Locations*. New York: Penguin Books, 2002

- Hillaire, Pauline. *A Totem Pole History: the Work of Lummi Carver Joe Hillaire*. Lincoln: University of Nebraska Press, 2013

- Hines, Harvey Kimball. *An Illustrated History of the State of Washington: Containing Biographical Mention of Its Pioneers and Prominent Citizens.* Chicago: Lewis Publishing Company, 1893

- Jackson, Terry, John Wade, and Wally Botsford. *Fishermen and Fisheries of the San Juan Islands: Those Were the Good Ole' Days.* Friday Harbor: 2011

- Jacobin, Louis. *With the Colors from Whatcom, Skagit and San Juan Counties: an Honor Roll Containing a Pictorial Record of the Gallant and Courageous Men from Northwestern Washington, U.S.A., Who Served in the World War, 1917-1918-1919.* Seattle: Peters Publishing Company, 1921

- Jeffcott, Percival R. *Nooksack Tales and Trails.* Ferndale, Washington: Whatcom County Pioneer Association, 1949

- Jones-Lamb, Karen. *Native American Wives of San Juan Settlers.* Eastsound: B. Tirion Publishing, 1994

- Keith, Gordon. *Voices from the Islands.* Portland: Binford & Mort, 1982

- LeBlond, Paul H. and Edward L. Bousfield. *Cadborosaurus: Survivor from the Deep.* Victoria: Heritage House Publishing, 2000

- Lindsay, F.W. *The B.C. Outlaws.* Kelowna, British Columbia: Regatta City Press, 1967

BIBLIOGRAPHY

- Long, James K. *Another Day in Paradise: Island Memories from the Thirties and Forties*. West Linn, Oregon: Long Publishing, 2002

- Ludwig, Charles H. *A Brief History of Waldron Island*. Seattle: 1959

- MacDonald, Margaret Read. *Ghost Stories of the Pacific Northwest*. Atlanta: August House, 1995

- McDonald, Lucile Saunders. *Making History: The People Who Shaped the San Juan Islands*. Friday Harbor: Harbor Press, 1990.

- McLachlan, Edith. *They Named It Deer Harbor*. Concrete, Washington: Concrete Herald Publishing Company, 1972

- McLellan, Roy Davison. *The Geology of the San Juan Islands*. Seattle: University of Washington Press, 1927

- Meany, Edmond S. *Origin of Washington Geographic Names*. Seattle: University of Washington Press, 1923

- Morgan, C.T. *The San Juan Story*. Friday Harbor: San Juan Industries, 1966

- Mueller, Marge and Ted Mueller. *The San Juan Islands, Afoot & Afloat*. Seattle: Mountaineers

Publishing, 1979

- Newell, Gordon R. *Ships of the Inland Sea*. Portland: Binfords & Mort, 1951

- O'Neill, Irene Barfoot, editor. *125 Years: Olga Memories and Potlucks*. Olga: 1996

- Orcas Island Historical Society and Museum. *Orcas Island*. Charleston, South Carolina: Arcadia Publishing, 2006

- Peacock, Christopher M. *Rosario Yesterdays*. Eastsound: Rosario Productions, 1985

- Pratt, Boyd C. *Lime: Quarrying and Limemaking in the San Juan Islands*. Friday Harbor: Mulno Cove Publications, 2016

- Reigel, Joseph W. *Shipwrecks of the San Juans*. Eastsound: Orcas Island History Press, 2024

- Riccio, Dolores and Joan Bingham. *Haunted Houses U.S.A.*. New York: Pocket Books, 1989

- Richardson, David. *This Is Our Story: Orcas Island Community Church from 1884 to the New Millennium*. Salt Lake City: Publishers Press, 1999

- Richardson, David. *Magic Islands: A Treasure-Trove of San Juan Islands Lore*. Eastsound: Orcas

Publishing Company, 1995

- Richardson, David. *Pig War Islands.* Eastsound: Orcas Publishing Company, 1990

- Roe, JoAnn. *The San Juan Islands: Into the 21st Century.* Caldwell, Idaho: Caxton Press, 2011

- Ruby, Robert H., and John A. Brown. *A Guide to the Indian Tribes of the Pacific Northwest.* Norman, Oklahoma: University of Oklahoma Press, 1992

- Schmoe, Floyd. *For Love of Some Islands.* New York: Harper & Row, 1964

- Splitstone, Fred John. *Orcas: Gem of the San Juans.* Sedro-Woolley, Washington: The Courier-Times Press, 1946

- "Spooks on Orcas Island." *Friday Harbor Journal,* February 23, 1922

- Stern, Bernhard J. *The Lummi Indians of North-west Washington.* New York: Columbia University Press, 1934

- Suttles, Wayne. *The Economic Life of the Coast Salish of Haro and Rosario Straits.* New York: Garland Publishing, 1974

- *The San Juan Islands: Illustrated Supplement to the San Juan Islander.* Friday Harbor: 1901

- Tillman, Thomas T. *Timeline of Orcas Island History*. Olga: Whalestooth Publishing, 1992

- *Told By The Pioneers: Tales of Frontier Life As Told by Those Who Remember the Days of the Territory and Early Statehood of Washington*. (3 vols). Olympia: Washington Pioneer Project, 1937-1938

- Tulloch, James F. *The James Francis Tulloch Diary*. Edited by Gordon Keith. Portland: Binford & Mort, 1978

- Varner, Gary R. *Creatures in the Mist: Little People, Wild Men and Spirit Beings around the World, a Study in Comparative Mythology*. New York: Algora Publishing, 2007

- Vosper, Lloyd. *Cruising Puget Sound and Adjacent Waters*. Seattle: Westward Press, 1947

- Wagner, Henry R. *Spanish Explorations in the Strait of Juan de Fuca*. Santa Ana, California: Fine Arts Press, 1933

- Walsh, Sophie. *History and Romance of the San Juan Islands*. Anacortes, Washington: Anacortes American Press, 1932

- Warren, James R. *The War Years: A Chronicle of Washington State in World War II*. Seattle: History Ink, 2000.

- Wellman, Candace. *Man of Treacherous Charm: Territorial Justice Edmund C. Fitzhugh.* Pullman, Washington: Washington State University Press, 2023

- Wilkes, Charles. *Narrative of the United States Exploring Expedition.* Philadelphia: 1850

- Wright, E.W., editor. *Lewis & Dryden's Marine History of the Pacific Northwest.* Portland: Lewis & Dryden Printing Company, 1895.

ARTICLES

- "A Dog's Love for Orcas Island." *Fairhaven Herald*, March 20, 1892

- Allen, Ethan. "Another Theory for Building of Anchor." *Friday Harbor Journal*, October 20, 1932

- "A Mountain Tragedy." *San Juan Islander*, June 30, 1911

- "A New Mining District." *The Islander*, March 25, 1897

- "A Queer Justice." *Puget Sound Mail*, April 1, 1882

- Bagby, Cali. "Ghosts on island?" *Islands' Sounder*, October 23, 2014

- Bourasaw, Noel V. "John Fravel, pioneer of both Whatcom and Skagit County." *Skagit River Journal of History & Folklore*, 2005

- Bousfield, Edward L. and Paul H. LeBlond. "An account of *Cadborosaurus willsi*, new genus, new species, a large aquatic reptile from the Pacific coast of North America." *Amphipacifica Vol. 1*, 1995, pp. 1-25

- Burn, June. "Visit to Olga." Puget Soundings, *Bellingham Herald*, January 16, 1930

- Burn, June. "Visit to Eastsound." Puget Soundings, *Bellingham Herald*, January 21, 1930

- Coleman, Edward T. "Mountaineering on the Pacific." *Harper's New Monthly Magazine*, November 1869

- Colmery, Carrell J. "Jim Baker Sights Sea Serpent On North Shore Of Orcas In May, 1909." *Orcas Islander*, September 1, 1962

- Cook, Beatrice. "Sage of the San Juans." *Pacific Motor Boat*, January 1939

- "Correction—We were misinformed as to the

name of the party who committed suicide at Orcas Island." *Northwest Enterprise*, September 2, 1882

- Craven, Robert. "A Brief History of Camp Orkila." YMCA of Seattle, May 1949

- "Young Man Drowned While In Swimming." *Friday Harbor Journal*, August 11, 1932

- "Defending Orcas Island." History Corner, *Orcas Islander*, October 28, 2010

- Deming, Elva Hanway. "A Homesteader's Recollections of Olga." *Orcas Islander*, July 12, 1944

- Dennis, Philip. "Ramtha 'speaking' to a new flock on Orcas." *Journal of the San Juans*, November 26, 1986

- Dickinson, Jeanne. "The Madrona Point Controversy." *The Planet*, Winter, Volume 10, Issue 2, 1989

- "Did Pinneo have a Pipe Dream?" *San Juan Islander*, November 26, 1903

- Dietrich, William. "A Century With Kids." *Seattle Times*, June 9, 2006

- "Ella Higginson's Bear 'Higgy' at Olga Inn." *San*

UNUSUAL ORCAS ISLAND

Juan Islander, July 8, 1910

- "Explorers Examine Mount Constitution's Wonderful Cave." *Anacortes American*, July 10, 1890

- "First Man to Report Flying Discs Guests at Olympic Lodge." *Orcas Islander*, July 29, 1948

- "Flying Disc Gets to Orcas At Long Last." *Orcas Islander*, July 24, 1947

- Geoghegan, Jack. "Observations by a Former Orcas Resident—Statements Corrected Relative to Pioneer Life." *Friday Harbor Journal*, February 27, 1930

- Geoghegan, Jack. "Orcas Island History Statements Correct." *Friday Harbor Journal*, May 8, 1930

- Giffin, W.R. "A Question—How Did Grindstone Bay Orcas Island Get Its Name?" *Friday Harbor Journal*, January 10, 1935

- Giffin, W.R. "Mysterious Stone Anchor on Mount-ain Top, Relic of Past." *Orcas Islander*, June 13, 1940

- Giffin, W.R. "Nine Families Settled at Mountain Lake, About 1890." *Orcas Islander*, June 6, 1940

- Giffin, W.R. "Shipwreck, Piracy or Whatnot:

For-gotten Story of the Past." *Friday Harbor Journal*, October 13, 1932

• Grossman, Ted. "Orcas tensions ease." *Islands' Sounder*, August 16, 1989

• "Held on Assault Charge." *Friday Harbor Journal*, October 5, 1922

• Hilen, Andrew. "Murder on Shaw Island." *Pacific Northwest Quarterly*, Vol. 69, No. 3, July 1978, pp. 97-106

• "Huge Grizzly Killed On Orcas Island." *San Juan Islander*, June 27, 1913

• Hutt, Sherry. "Notice of Inventory Completion: Thomas Burke Memorial Washington State Museum, University of Washington, Seattle, WA." Department of the Interior, 2012

• "Indian Murderers." *Seattle Daily Post-Intelligencer*, January 8, 1884

• Kimple, Woodsy. "Kimple Tells Story of Island's Sea Serpents and of Blackfish." *Orcas Islander*, October 1, 1954

• "King Solomon's Mines Not In It: 'Mountain of Gold-Bearing Ore' on Orcas Island." *San Juan Islander*, April 14, 1906

- Koltun, Jan. "Civil War Veteran, Master Carpenter: Michael Donohue," History Nook, *Islands' Sounder*, July 2, 2014

- Langell, Wes. "Langell Family Settled on Orcas Isl-and 75 Years Ago." *Orcas Islander*, November 30, 1944

- Larson, Heather. "Hauntingly familiar." *Spokesman-Review*, October 28, 2007

- "Lost Mail: Why Our Letters and Newspapers Never Reach Their Destination." *Whatcom Reveille*, August 24th, 1883

- "Lummi Indian Falls From Bluff to his Death." *Bellingham Herald*, February 18, 1909

- Mapes, Diane. "When guest meets ghost: Orcas Hotel and other supernatural sleeps." *Seattle Times*, October 31, 2002

- McAbee, Clark. "Orcas Island gets a Colonel." Hist-ory Nook, *Islands' Sounder*, 2018

- McDonald, Lucile Saunders. "Kelly, the King of the Smugglers: Guemes, Sinclair Islands were head-quarters of notorious operator in years long past." *Seattle Times*, March 29, 1959

- McDonald, Lucile Saunders. "San Juan Limestone Resources." *Seattle Times*, September 13, 1959

- McDonald, Lucile Saunders. "Tracking the Smugglers." *Seattle Times*, July 27, 1952

- "Murder and Robbery." *Weekly Pacific Tribune*, April 17, 1878

- "Murder in Second Degree: Robertson Sentenced to Fifteen Years Imprisonment—Verdict Reached After Over Four Hours Deliberation." *San Juan Islander*, May 1, 1902

- "Murder Near Olga: 'Jack' Hand Shot and Instantly Killed by Tom Robertson." *San Juan Islander*, February 20, 1902

- "Napoleon in Olga?" History Corner, *Orcas Islander*, December 7, 2010

- "Nearly Half a Century Spent at His Home in Beautiful Olga: John Gray, Pioneer of Orcas Island, Built His Cabin Forty Years Ago from Lumber Hand-sawed on Samish Flats." *Anacortes American*, July 8, 1911

- "Nice Little Joke on Wm. Moran: Mineral Claims Reported Filed By 'Enterprising Islanders' Upon Some of His Property at Cascade Lake."

San Juan Islander, May 12, 1906

- "Odd Fellows Hall at East Sound Destroyed." *Friday Harbor Journal*, January 5, 1950

- "Odd Fellows Start Work on New Hall; Everyone Helps on Project." *Orcas Islander*, September 21, 1950

- "Olga Merchant Takes Own Life in Fit of Despondency." *Friday Harbor Journal*, February 8, 1934

- "Orcas Island Gold Mine." *San Juan Islander*, March 8, 1900

- "Orcas Island Sanitarium: May Be Established at the Sulphur Springs." *San Juan Islander*, December 24, 1904

- "Orcas Island, Washington." *The West Shore: The Great Pacific Coast Illustrated Weekly*, Vol. 16, 1890

- "Outlaw Cave is Discovered: Barnes Island in San Juan Group Gives Up Secret of Smuggler Bands That Once Plied Trade There." *Anacortes American*, January 28, 1915

- "Peculiar Relic Is Found on Orcas Island." *Anacortes American*, July 10, 1924

- "Pioneer of Orcas Island Dies." *Friday Harbor*

Journal, May 27, 1913

- "Pioneer Orcas Man Summoned." *Friday Harbor Journal*, May 14, 1936

- "*Prelude* Disaster Remains a Riddle." *Bellingham Herald*, March 26, 1965

- Richardson, David. "Moran Park Gold 'Diggings.'" *Islands' Sounder*, July 27, 1983

- Richardson, David. "Turtleback Mountain's Mysterious 'Anchor'." *Orcas Sounder*, June 17, 1966

- "Rich Orcas Gold Mines: Nickel, Gold and Silver in Paying Quantities." *Seattle Post-Intelligencer*, October 23, 1899

- "Robertson Pleads Not Guilty, Demands Jury Trial." *Friday Harbor Journal*, October 12, 1922

- "Robertson Up For Trial." *Friday Harbor Journal*, November 9, 1922

- "Rumblings From Mt. Constitution's Gold Mine." *Islands' Sounder*, September 4, 1985

- "Sad Holiday Ending For Bellingham Fishermen." *Friday Harbor Journal*, September 6, 1945

- "San Juan County, Washington: San Juan, Orcas,

and Lopez Isles." *The Coast - Wilhelm's Magazine*, June, 1903

- "Sensation on Orcas Island." *Northwest Enterprise*, April 15, 1882

- Shapley, Tom and Deborah M. Smith. "Close Encounters?" *Journal of the San Juans*, February 21, 1978

- Shattuck, B.F. "First Store in Eastsound Owned By Chas. Shattuck." *Orcas Islander*, December 14, 1944

- Smith, Colleen. "Madrona Point: 20 years of Lummi ownership; Orcas community still denied access." *Islands' Sounder*, February 18, 2010

- Smith, Deborah M. "Journal Investigates UFO Hoax Theory." *Journal of the San Juans*, February 24, 1978

- "Some Mysteries of Mt. Constitution." *San Juan Islander*, February 2, 1912

- Sorenson, Eric. "San Juan 'Gem' Sparkles in Soli-tude." *Seattle Times*, June 2, 2003

- " 'Spelunkers' Visit Orcas Island." *Orcas Islander*, January 1, 1961

BIBLIOGRAPHY

- Steinkopf, Alvin. "Four Winds Campers Sail to Europe." *Seattle Times*, February 15, 1950

- Stumbo, Stacy D. "Artifacts found during East-sound street project." *Journal of the San Juans*, April 14, 1999

- "The Archipelago De Haro: A Lovely Spot in the Straits of Fuca." *Seattle Post-Intelligencer*, January 1, 1891

- "The Great Orcas Island Bear Hunt," History Corner, *Orcas Islander*, November 8, 2011

- "The Legend of Indian George Lives On." *Orcas Sounder*, August 4, 1966

- "The Olga Tragedy: Robertson's Voluntary Statement to the Islander as to 'the Cause of the Altercation." *San Juan Islander*, February 27, 1902

- "The Smuggler's Pride: The Brief History of Kelly the Smuggler and His Boat." *Fairhaven Herald*, July 29, 1891

- Thrush, Coll-Peter, and Robert H. Keller, Jr. "'I See What I Have Done': The Life and Murder Trial of Xwelas, a S'Klallam Woman." *Western Historical Quarterly*, Vol. 26, No. 2, Summer, 1995, pp. 168-183

- "Times Article Recalls Island's Famous Murder." *Orcas Islander*, October 1, 1959

- "Tom Robertson Given Term at Walla Walla." *Friday Harbor Journal*, February 8, 1923

- "Tom Robertson Found Guilty." *Friday Harbor Journal*, December 14, 1922

- "Tragedy on Orcas: Thomas Robertson Shoots and Kills John Hand." *Fairhaven Herald*, February 18, 1902

- "Tribute of Respect." *Puget Sound Mail*, July 22, 1882

- Tulloch, James F. "Former Resident Answers Questions." *Friday Harbor Journal*, April 10, 1930

- " 'Ugly Elsie' Alive & Well Near Victoria." *Orcas Island Booster*, March 1, 1970

- "UW Student to Explore Orcas." *Anacortes American*, November 2, 1950

- Vollmer, Jen. "The History of Moran State Park." *Islands' Weekly*, October 2000

- Waldman, Peter. "New Age divides oldtimers on island." *Journal of the San Juans*, October 26, 1988

- Walsh, Sophie. "Adventures of Childhood." *Anacortes American*, April 3, 1930

- Walsh, Sophie. "Sea Creature Is Victim of Lone Raider On Orcas." *Anacortes American*, November 13, 1930

- Walsh, Sophie. "Orcas history." Shanghaied on Orcas. *Anacortes American*, January 16, 1930

- Walsh, Sophie. "Walsh's Philippine collection." Shanghaied on Orcas. *Anacortes American*, November 21, 1929

- Walsh, Sophie. "More of Walsh's Moro curios." Shanghaied on Orcas. *Anacortes American*, January 9, 1930

- Welch, Tom. *"Dirty Elsie."* History Corner, *Orcas Islander*, September 18, 2013

- "Well Known Orcas Island Resident Commits Suicide." *Friday Harbor Journal*, July 8, 1915

- "What Do You Know?" *Friday Harbor Journal*, January 6, 1938

- "When Orcas Had a Wild Man." *Orcas Islander*, May 7, 1941

- Wilhelm, Steven. "Cultivating human potentials

on Orcas." *Friday Harbor Journal*, November 25, 1981

- "'Yellow' Story of Smuggling: The facts About the Recent Seizure of A Sloop Here." *San Juan Islander*, December 14, 1907

Index